D0363737

SUE KREITZMAN'S

LOW-FAT DESSERTS

Sue Kreitzman, described by *The Times* as 'the queen of low-fat cookery writing', wholeheartedly believes in good food with maximum flavour and minimum fat.

Sue lectures and demonstrates all around the country, and regularly appears on radio and television. She contributes to many national magazines and newspapers, including *BBC Good Food, Woman's Own, Woman's Realm, Living* and the *Mail on Sunday*.

Sue Kreitzman's Low Fat Desserts is her twenty-second book. Her other books include *Sue Kreitzman's Complete Low Fat Cookbook, Sue Kreitzman's Low Fat Vegetarian Cookbook, The Low Fat Cookbook, The Quick After-Work Low Fat Cookbook, Lavish Low-Fat Cooking, Slim Cuisine Italian Style* and *Slim Cuisine Quick and Easy.*

SUE KREITZMAN'S
LOW-FAT DESSERTS

PIATKUS

First published in 1998 by
Judy Piatkus (Publishers) Ltd
5 Windmill Street
London W1P 1HF

www.piatkus.co.uk

This paperback edition published in 1999

The moral right of the author has been asserted

A catalogue record for this book is available from the British Library

ISBN 0 7499 1861 6 (hbk)
     0 7499 1972 8 (pbk)

Cover design by Button Design shows Yogurt and
Ricotta Cream Berry Tart with Apricot Glaze (p. 47),
Killer Chocolate Chestnut Layer Cake (p. 112) and
Meringue Layer Torte (p. 63)
Food preparation by Emma Patmore
Styling by Marian Price

Text designed by Jerry Goldie
Photography by Ian O'Leary
Food preparation by Janice Murfitt
Styling by Marian Price
Nutritional analysis by Jasmine Challis

Typeset by Wyvern 21, Bristol
Printed and bound in Great Britain by
Butler & Tanner Ltd, Frome and London

Nutritional analysis

All nutritional figures given are approximate
and should be used as a guide. They are
based on data from food tables or from
manufacturers data rather than by direct
analysis. The symbol <1G in the analyses
means the recipe quantity analysed contains
less than 1 gram of the fat named. **Neg**
(negligible) means 0.1g or 0.2g of fat.

Contents

FOR HEATHER ROCKLIN

Heather, I'll miss you – it has been a real pleasure working together these last few years. *Good* luck and much joy to you, Keith and Ralph Milo. Thanks to Rachel Winning for stepping in with grace and efficiency, and many affectionate thanks to Judy Piatkus for impelling me into the low-fat cheesecake adventure. Loving thanks to my family, Steve and Shawm, for the fun we have, and to the Roman Road network including Keith Brewster and Peter Novis; Peter King and Katie Ashley; Jeanette Hoare and Googie Woodham; my friends at Roman Cars who tasted several desserts with heartwarming enthusiasm, and provided valuable comments; and all the rest of the Roman Road cast of characters who make life in this little piece of London such a pleasure.

Janet Tod and Graeme Douglas provide constant practical input on the usefulness of my techniques and recipes, and Janet enriches my life with intense helpings of art, colour and gardening know how – who could possibly ask for anything more?

The Fairman clan are supportive, lively and infinitely kind neighbours; sometimes I almost feel like a member of the family. My young neighbours Joe and Thomas (along with Luke, Ben, Danielle, and rest of the Hitchin Square children) keep life exceptionally interesting, and Toby provides unconditional canine adoration.

My friend Marlena Spieler's food sings with sunshine, warmth, and pizzazz; she and Alan McLaughlan have provided many hours of shared laughter, good food and conversation.

Mandy Morton and I continue to sustain our Saturday radio conversations with fluency, hilarity and ease – I'm not sure how we do it, but I sure enjoy the hell out of it!

Nina Myskow has been an elegant and wonderful foil, and a pleasure to work with on Granada Sky's "Eat, Drink and be Healthy", and she has been generous and enthusiastic about my work.

David Grossman provides professional wisdom, friendship and support in equal measure, Sandie Mitchel-King continues to keep things efficiently glued together on every level, Brenda Huebler, as always, keeps it all clean and tidy, and Trudy Stevenson has stepped in to provide invaluable help.

The photography team of Ian O'Leary at the lens and Janice Murfitt in the kitchen have performed their usual magic – and Janice provided a valuable suggestion about meringue in the tea loaves.

Thank you all, I couldn't do it without you.

INTRODUCTION

There is a prevailing notion that a low-fat regime means austerity, meanness, boredom and an end to the sensual enjoyment of food. What piffle! In fact, cutting down on fat unlocks flavour in a most astonishing way; suddenly your palate revels in the strong bright flavours of food as it is unveiled of its muffling layers of fats and oils. Low-fat desserts are especially revelatory – rich, creamy, even deeply chocolatey, but never cloying or heavy.

I have been a champion of low-fat gastronomy for years now, but still, no matter what I say, doubters continue to doubt, until I feed them my cheesecake, my tiramisù or my chocolate and raspberry trifle, then they decide that I'm either a liar (this food *must* be high-fat) or a witch. Of course, witchcraft has nothing to do with it; it's just a question of understanding ingredients and techniques, and then letting your culinary imagination run free. Once you turn your passion for good food away from butter and cream, and towards healthy ingredients and techniques, there will be no stopping you.

I've tried to incorporate every kind of dessert into this collection: nostalgic nursery puddings; light fruit desserts; substantial cheesecakes; chocolate seductions; cream-filled cakes; the exotically foreign and the comfortingly domestic. Many are very low-fat and some are medium-fat adaptations of frighteningly high-fat originals. To make things easier, each recipe is analysed for Calorie and fat values and – where appropriate – the fat and Calorie values for the originals are included as well. That's where the real fun is: check out the cheesecake and the tiramisù for dramatic examples of the fat and Calorie savings possible

when you switch to my methods. Are the original versions
really worth 43 extra grams of fat (the cheesecake) or 32
grams (the tiramisù) *per serving*? I think not: my versions
are swooningly delicious without the fat whammy, but then
I *would* say that. You must try these fabulously lightened
new-wave recipes, and decide for yourself.

Ingredients

Making low-fat desserts means taking a fresh look at
traditional dessert ingredients, many of which are
notoriously high in fat. I use few whole eggs or egg yolks,
and no butter, margarine, cream or full-fat dairy products,
but you will find other wonderfully useful products to use
instead – not exact substitutes, but interesting ingredients
in their own right.

Oil and water spray

This delivers a fine mist of oil (a minuscule amount) and
water that nicely greases a pan. Buy a clean, new plastic
perfume spray atomiser or a small plant mister, and fill it
seven-eighths full with water and one-eighth full with
safflower or sunflower oil. To use, shake and spray.

Eggs

There is still plenty of scientific controversy surrounding the
blood cholesterol/dietary cholesterol puzzle. The prevailing
view seems to be that it is general dietary fat levels that
control blood cholesterol, rather than just high cholesterol
foods *per se*. An egg yolk is high in cholesterol but contains
just 5.2 grams of fat (for a large egg) along with plenty of
other nutrients, so an occasional whole egg shouldn't hurt.
(Of course, if you have high blood cholesterol levels or
arterial and heart problems, check with your doctor.) I use
the occasional whole egg in the recipes in this book, but not

in great quantity, and not very often. The whites are another story altogether. They are very low in fat and extraordinarily useful in dessert making.

Quark, very low-fat fromage frais, very low-fat yogurt

These are very useful cultured skimmed milk products available in most supermarkets. Quark spreads like cream cheese; fromage frais has a light, sour cream-like texture and is slightly tangy; very low-fat yogurt is thin, watery and sour. It can be drained to make it thick and creamy (see page 149) but it will still be quite tangy; this is no problem for yogurt fans. Quark and fromage frais are just fine as they are.

Ricotta cheese

Sweet, creamy and medium fat (14–15 per cent), ricotta makes a wonderful stand-in for scary high-fat ingredients such as crème fraîche, mascarpone and whipped cream (all at least 80 per cent fat). One brand of ricotta (Galbani) lists the fat content for 'dry matter' as 45 per cent. The actual fat percentage of the moist cheese, as purchased, is approximately 14 per cent, so don't worry, it is quite all right to use ricotta in low-fat desserts.

Low-fat soft cheese

With this low-fat version (approximately 6 per cent fat) of cream cheese you'll be able to make extremely low-fat cheesecakes that rival the high-fat originals. Read the labels and buy the soft cheese with the lowest fat level (less than 8 per cent).

Skimmed milk

Buy fresh skimmed milk for ice creams and milk puddings, and keep a few cartons of UHT ('ultra-high temperature'), that is 'long-life', skimmed milk in the cupboard. The UHT milk has a cooked taste, making it unsuitable for the ice cream recipes, but it is excellent in bread puddings. One carton is just the right amount for one bread pudding.

Skimmed milk powder

Add this to skimmed milk for extra richness (and improved nutrition).

Sweetened condensed skimmed milk

This comes in cans (make sure you choose skimmed; there is a full-fat version as well) and is thick, sweet and sticky – totally childish in fact. There is a popular recipe that turns up all over the world for boiling the sealed can for a long time, until the contents turn to caramel. This practice is, in fact, quite dangerous (the can is liable to explode) so don't try it at home. The milk, out of the can, gives amazing richness to all sorts of low-fat desserts, from ice creams to bread puddings.

Light evaporated milk

I wish that evaporated skimmed milk were available in the UK (perhaps one day it will be). Until it is, this, at 4 per cent fat, is not bad. It lends richness and a velvety texture to many puddings.

Sweeteners

There *is* life beyond sugar, especially in low-fat cooking, when you are trying to build depth of flavour. Sugar has its uses, but try a few other sweeteners as well – maple syrup, honey and marmalades, jams, conserves, and so on. I especially like the French no-added-sugar, high-fruit spreads available in jars in many supermarkets these days. They come in all sorts of flavours (apricot, blueberry, raspberry...) and make splendid sweeteners, at the same time adding flavour to all sorts of puddings and creams. When buying maple syrup, make sure it is *pure* maple syrup; honey should be mild and runny. Nutritionally speaking, these alternative sweeteners have no real advantage over sugar (they all are, after all, basically made from different sugars), but the complex and interesting flavours they contribute make them very valuable.

Wines and spirits

Liqueurs are used to add zing to several of the puddings in this book. In many cases, the alcohol is not cooked away, so be cautious about serving them to children. Dark rum is used a few times (dynamite with bananas), along with Cointreau, Tia Maria, sherry, red wine (for braising pears) and a host of others.

Dried fruit

The array of dried fruits on offer these days is staggering. In addition to the usual apricots, raisins, figs, prunes, and so on, look for cranberries, blueberries, cherries, mangoes, moist raisins (essentially pre-soaked – very good for puddings and baking) and, in wholefood shops, the stunning Hunza apricots (see page 146). Seek out, as well, 'Lighter Bake', a prune–apple purée in a jar, meant to be used as a fat substitute in baking (see page 28).

Citrus fruit

Citrus fruit zest is used constantly in desserts for its flavour and aroma. Use a zester (a little instrument with a stubby, perforated blade) and wield it so that some of the fragrant citrus oil goes into the recipe along with the zest. (If you haven't got a zester, grate the zest using the fine holes of a grater, but be sure to avoid grating the bitter white pith beneath the zest.) Buy unwaxed fruit, or scrub it well before removing the zest.

Vanilla extract

Buy the real thing – pure natural vanilla (available by mail order if necessary, see page 156). Use vanilla pods as well. Once you have split open a pod and scraped out the fragrant pulp, the pod can be placed in a jar of caster sugar and left to impart its flavour to the sugar.

Ginger

Crystallised ginger, snipped up finely with scissors, gives sweet, hot zip, and stem ginger in syrup gives a sweet gingery bite as well. The syrup itself is wonderful as a sweetener, with plenty of pizzazz.

Amaretti biscuits

Choose amaretti biscuits that are flavoured with apricot kernels rather than high-fat almonds (read the label to check). The amaretti that come in pairs in pretty paper wrappers are perfect.

Grape Nuts breakfast cereal

Look on the supermarket shelves for this crumbly American cereal, perfect for crumb crusts and crumble toppings.

Chocolate

One of life's major pleasures! How fortunate it is that homemade low-fat chocolate desserts can be so rich and pleasurable. Buy low-fat cocoa powder (available by mail order, if necessary, see page 156) and excellent quality (no vegetable fat) high-cocoa-solid (at least 60 per cent) dark chocolate.

Unsweetened chestnut purée

This is used in several of the recipes in this book to give body. Chestnuts are the only low-fat nut, and the purée delivers wonderful carbohydrate comfort. You'll find it in cans in the supermarket. None of the recipes that call for the purée use a complete can, so if you are going to make one of the ice creams, make the Chocolate Chestnut Filling or Spread (see page 116) as well, or use the remainder to make a savoury chestnut soup.

Equipment

Non-stick bakeware

Along with silicone baking parchment, non-stick baking tins are essential. A 23 cm (9 inch), and a 25.5 cm (10 inch) springform tin will enable you to bake gorgeous cheesecakes and tarts, but the tins must be of good quality; poorly made ones don't always seal well, and leak all over the place.

An angel cake tin is essential as well, so that you can produce the original truly fatless sponge – the Angel Cake. If you can't get the tins you need locally, a list of mail order addresses is given on page 156.

Basics

An accurate set of scales and a good selection of measuring spoons and jugs are indispensable in any kitchen. Also useful for low-fat dessert making are a nylon sieve, flexible rubber spatulas (for folding egg white mixtures and batters), whisks, a pair of kitchen scissors, a palette knife and – very important – a cake tester. You might also need to buy a new spray bottle for your oil and water spray (see page 10).

Machines

You will use a food processor (a small one is handy and efficient), a blender and a hand-held electric mixer again and again. They really do make life easier, and with a processor you will be able to produce instant ice cream (see page 89) any time you get the urge. A microwave is convenient (although not essential) as well, and allows you to prepare skimmed milk puddings without scorching.

Cleaning scorched pans

Skimmed milk catches very easily, so it is inevitable that the occasional disaster will occur and you will need to deal with a badly blackened saucepan. Soak it overnight in a slurry of water and biological washing powder; on the next day it should rinse clean.

Non-reactive cookware

Cast-iron, tin and aluminium cookware will react with acid ingredients, such as wine and some fruits, producing off-flavours and discolouration. To avoid these problems use *non-reactive* cookware, such as enamelled cast-iron, stainless steel or flameproof glass, or cookware with a non-stick coating.

CHAPTER 1

CAKES, ROULADES AND TEABREADS

A cake is the ultimate celebration dessert. Most cakes are butterfat nightmares (or, even worse, margarine nightmares), but, fortunately, there are plenty of techniques for low-fat or medium-fat cake making. I believe that healthy low-fat living is a lifetime commitment, and that includes birthdays, anniversaries, and other cake-worthy events. Next time you are celebrating, try one of the recipes in this chapter.

Angel Cake and Variations

Angel cake is an American classic, a towering gossamer soufflé-like cake, baked in a tube tin with a removable bottom. If you have any difficulty obtaining an angel cake tin, they are available by mail order (see page 156).

An angel cake is made with no fat whatsoever, no egg yolks, no greasing of the pan; just plenty of egg whites, a bit of cream of tartar to stabilise the whites, some sugar and flour. It is important that the egg whites have not a speck of yolk in them (and that the bowl and beaters are very clean) or they will not whip up into meringue.

The original angel cake is flavoured with vanilla, baked in the tube tin, and served very simply, with some berries, coulis, a drizzle of Chocolate Sauce (see page 117) or fruit compote. However, angel cakes can be varied in all sorts of ways: flavoured with chocolate, cinnamon or orange, or even baked flat to form a roulade or the base of a layer cake.

The flour available in the UK is less fine and soft than American cake flour, so an angel cake made here will never be quite as feathery light and melting as an American-made one, but I don't find this a problem. An American angel is actually rather insipid and insubstantial – made with British flour it has more body, more character, is slightly more compact and is ultimately more satisfying.

Black and White Angel Cake

CALORIE COUNT 129 KCAL FAT CONTENT <0.5G PER SLICE

The best of both worlds: chocolate *and* vanilla in one cake.

90 g (3 oz) plain flour

270 g (9 oz) caster sugar

3 tablespoons low-fat unsweetened cocoa powder

10 egg whites (at room temperature)

pinch of cream of tartar

1 1/2 teaspoons natural vanilla extract

Makes one 25 cm (10 inch) cake; 12 slices

1 Preheat the oven to 190°C, 375°F, Gas Mark 5.
2 Sift 60g (2 oz) of the flour and 45 g (1 1/2 oz) of the sugar together into a bowl and set aside.
3 Sift the remaining flour, the cocoa powder and 60 g (2 oz) of the remaining sugar together into another bowl and set aside.
4 Put the egg whites in a large bowl with the cream of tartar and beat with an electric mixer until they hold soft peaks. Beat in the remaining sugar, 2 tablespoons at a time, until the sugar is dissolved and the whites are stiff and glossy and hold firm peaks. Fold in the vanilla.
5 Spoon half the meringue into another bowl and fold in the white flour/sugar mixture. Fold the cocoa/flour mixture into the remaining half of the meringue.
6 Gently spoon and push the white meringue into an ungreased angel cake tin 25 cm (10 inch) diameter, 10 cm (4 inches) deep. Spoon and push the chocolate batter evenly over the white. Bake in the oven for 30–35 minutes. The cake is done when it springs back if gently pressed with your finger, and a cake tester comes out clean when inserted gently into the cake. The surface of the cake is likely to be cracked, like a soufflé.
7 Cool *upside-down* by inverting the cake, in its tin, over a bottle (the neck of the bottle should come right up through the tube), or on an inverted funnel. Leave for *at least* 1 hour.
8 Use a long palette knife to loosen the cake gently around the sides and bottom of the tin, and around the tube. Gently shake, and turn on to a plate. To serve, cut gently, using a sawing motion, with a long, sharp, serrated knife.

Vanilla Angel Cake

CALORIE COUNT 133 KCAL FAT CONTENT <0.5G PER SLICE

Ten egg whites will whip up to an impressive volume, so use a *large* bowl. It is important to use the best pure vanilla extract you can find. Use electric beaters, or you will suffer from angel cake-elbow for weeks!

125 g (4 oz) plain flour
275 g (9 oz) caster sugar
10 egg whites (at room temperature)
pinch of cream of tartar
1¹/₂ teaspoons natural vanilla extract

Makes one 25 cm (10 inch cake); 12 slices

1 Preheat the oven to 190°C, 375°F, Gas Mark 5.
2 Sift together the flour and 105 g (3¹/₂ oz) of the sugar together into a bowl and set aside.
3 Put the egg whites in a large bowl and beat with an electric mixer until foamy. Add the cream of tartar and beat until the egg whites hold soft peaks. Continue beating, adding the remaining 165 g (5¹/₂ oz) sugar, 2 tablespoons at a time, until the sugar is dissolved, and the whites are stiff and glossy. Fold in the vanilla.
4 A little at a time, sprinkle the sifted flour/sugar mixture over the egg whites and fold in gently but thoroughly.
5 Gently spoon and push the meringue into an ungreased 25 cm (10 inch) diameter, 10 cm (4 inches) deep angel cake tube tin. Bake in the oven for 30–35 minutes. When it is done, the top will most likely have cracked like a soufflé, the cake will spring back when gently pressed with your finger, and a cake tester will come out clean when inserted gently into the cake.
6 Cool *upside-down* by inverting the cake, in its tin, over a bottle (the neck of the bottle should come right up through the tube), or on an inverted funnel. (Some angel cake tins have small 'feet' around the rim on which to stand the upside-down tin while the cake cools.) Leave for *at least* 1 hour.
7 Use a long palette knife to loosen the cake gently around the sides and bottom of the tin, and around the tube. Gently shake, and turn out on to a plate. To serve, cut gently, using a sawing motion, with a long, sharp, serrated knife.

Angel Cake Variations

Spiced Angel

Sift a small amount (1/8–1/4 teaspoon) of ground spice into the flour in step 2. Choose nutmeg, cinnamon or mixed spice.

Citrus-Scented Angel

Fold some grated orange, lemon or lime zest into the beaten egg whites.

Other Possible Flavours

Use almond extract or rosewater in place of the vanilla extract.

Chocolate Angel Cake

A chocolate angel is splendid, not only as it is (served with some fresh raspberries, perhaps, and a scoop of Chocolate Sorbet, see page 99), but cubed and used as the base of an over-the-top trifle (see pages 55 6).

Reduce the amount of flour to 90 g (3 oz) and, in step 2, sift 6 tablespoons low-fat unsweetened cocoa powder with the sugar and flour.

Separating Eggs

Eggs are easiest to separate when still cold, but the whites whip up to maximum volume when at room temperature. To make your baking life easier, separate the yolks from the whites, then stand them (in their bowl) in a larger bowl of warm water. It won't take long for them to warm to room temperature.

Angel Layer Cakes and Roulades

A flat-baked angel sheet can be cut into two or three pieces, then sandwiched one on top of the other with a filling, and glazed or iced. Alternatively, the sheet can be left uncut, spread with a creamy filling, and rolled to form a roulade. These layer cakes and roulades are not compromises in any sense; although low fat they taste as festive and satisfying as any traditional confection.

Vanilla Angel Sheet Cake

CALORIE COUNT 813 KCAL FAT CONTENT 1G PER WHOLE CAKE

60 g (2 oz) plain flour
140 g (4½ oz) caster sugar
5 egg whites (at room temperature)
pinch of cream of tartar
1½ teaspoons natural vanilla extract

Makes one 33 x 23 cm (13 x 9 inch) sheet cake

1 Preheat the oven to 180°C, 350°F, Gas Mark 4. Line a 33 x 23 cm (13 x 9 inch) Swiss roll tin with baking parchment.
2 Sift the flour and 75 g (2½ oz) of the sugar together into a bowl and set aside.
3 Put the egg whites in a large bowl and beat with an electric mixer until foamy. Add the cream of tartar and beat until the egg whites hold soft peaks. Continue beating, adding the remaining 60 g (2 oz) sugar, 2 tablespoons at a time, until the sugar is dissolved, and the whites are stiff and glossy. Fold in the vanilla.
4 A little at a time, sprinkle the sifted flour and sugar mixture over the egg whites, and fold in gently but thoroughly.
5 Gently spoon the meringue into the prepared tin and bake in the oven for 10–15 minutes or until the sponge springs back when gently pressed with your finger, and a cake tester inserted in the centre comes out clean. Leave to cool in the tin on a wire rack.

Chocolate Angel Sheet Cake

CALORIE COUNT 824 KCAL FAT CONTENT 4G PER WHOLE CAKE

This Chocolate Sheet Cake, cut into 2 or 3 parts and filled, or filled, rolled and iced, will delight you and those you feed whether you decide to make the outrageously creamy Hungarian (de-fatted) Rigo Jancsi (page 25), the Chocolate Ginger Roulade (page 27) or the wonderfully festive Bûche de Noel (page 138).

45 g (1½ oz) plain flour
3 tablespoons low-fat unsweetened cocoa powder
140 g (4½ oz) caster sugar
5 egg whites (at room temperature)
pinch of cream of tartar
1 teaspoon natural vanilla extract

Makes one 33 x 23 cm (13 x 9 inch) sheet cake

1 Preheat the oven to 180°C, 350°F, Gas Mark 4. Line a 33 x 23 cm (13 x 9 inch) Swiss roll tin with baking parchment.
2 Sift the flour, cocoa and 75 g (2½ oz) of the sugar together into a bowl and set aside.
3 Put the egg whites in a large bowl and beat with an electric mixer until foamy. Add the cream of tartar and beat until the egg whites hold soft peaks. Continue beating, adding the remaining sugar, 2 tablespoons at a time, until the sugar is dissolved and the whites are stiff and glossy. Fold in the vanilla.
4 A little at a time, sprinkle the sifted flour and sugar mixture over the egg whites and fold in gently but thoroughly.
5 Gently spoon the mixture into the prepared tin and bake in the oven for 10–15 minutes or until the sponge springs back when gently pressed with your finger, and a cake tester inserted in the centre comes out clean. Leave to cool in the tin on a wire rack.

Raspberry Sandwich Torte

CALORIE COUNT 173 KCAL FAT CONTENT 5G PER SERVING

Chocolate and raspberries are fabulous together, so this
would be equally good made using the chocolate sheet cake
(see page 23). Why not try it with strawberries or
blueberries for a change? The strawberries would work well
with either the vanilla or the chocolate layers, but
blueberries should be used with vanilla sponge only. In each
case, seek out the appropriate fruit spread; both strawberry
and blueberry are available.

one Vanilla Angel Sheet Cake (page 22)

Filling
275 g (9 oz) carton ricotta
1 tablespoon no-added-sugar, high-fruit raspberry spread
1 teaspoon Cointreau
1¹/₂ teaspoons natural vanilla extract
150 g (5 oz) fresh raspberries
1 heaped tablespoon finely grated high-cocoa-solid dark
    chocolate (see Note, below)

Serves 8

1 For the filling, put the ricotta and raspberry spread in a food processor and
  process until well combined.
2 When the sheet cake is cool, carefully turn it out of the tin and peel off the
  lining paper. Cut the cake in half down the centre to form two square layers.
  Put one half on a plate. Combine the Cointreau and vanilla and sprinkle over
  the cake halves.
3 Spread the half of the cake on a plate with the ricotta mixture, top with the
  fresh raspberries in an even layer, sprinkle with half of the chocolate, and place
  the second cake half on top with the more attractive side facing up. Sprinkle
  with the remaining grated chocolate. Refrigerate until needed. To serve, cut
  into squares.

Note
Grate the chocolate almost to a powder using the fine holes on a grater.

Rigo Jancsi

CALORIE COUNT 144 KCAL FAT CONTENT 3G PER SERVING   (TRADITIONAL RECIPE CALORIE COUNT 508 KCAL FAT CONTENT 38G)

I have been a devotee of Hungarian cooking for years, and have – at this point – a large repertoire of low-fat versions of lots of killer traditional recipes (it is a *very* high-fat cuisine). I first ate Rigo Jancsi (chocolate-cream-filled squares) on my honeymoon, 36 years ago, and I still think it's one of the best celebration chocolate desserts in the world. Reducing the fat levels has not harmed its seductiveness one bit.

one Chocolate Angel Sheet Cake (page 23)

about 1/2 quantity Chocolate Ricotta Mousse (page 116)

1 tablespoon finely grated high-cocoa-solid dark chocolate (see Note on page 24)

Makes 12 slices

1 When the sheet cake is cool, carefully turn it out of the tin and peel off the lining paper. Cut the cake in half down the centre to form two square layers. Put one half on a serving plate and spread it with the Chocolate Ricotta Mousse. Top with the second half, the more attractive side up.
2 Sprinkle the grated chocolate evenly on top. Refrigerate until needed.

'... the Chocolate Elite – the select millions who like chocolate in all its infinite varieties, using "like" as in "I like to breathe".'

Sandra Boynton; *Chocolate, The Consuming Passion*

Cannoli-Cream-Filled Layer Cake

CALORIE COUNT 139 KCAL FAT CONTENT 2G PER SLICE   (TRADITIONAL RECIPE CALORIE COUNT 241 KCAL FAT CONTENT 12G)

Cannoli are cornets of fried dough filled with a rich cream studded with candied fruit. Years ago I used to buy them in the North End of Boston in one of the marvellous Italian pastry shops that thrived in that area. They were absolutely gorgeous, but wickedly high-fat. This cake brings back all of the memories, but only a fraction of the fat. You could make this cake with any of the creams on pages 150–54. Change the glaze to complement the filling, or use the Chocolate Chestnut Filling or Spread (see page 116) and lavish it over the top and sides of the cake with a palette knife.

> one Vanilla Angel Sheet Cake (page 22)
> 2–3 tablespoons orange-flavoured liqueur or
>   Amaretto di Saronno
> about ¹/₂ quantity Cannoli Cream (page 153)
> Marmalade Glaze (page 154)

Makes 12 slices

1 When the sheet cake is cool, carefully turn it out of the tin and peel off the lining paper. Cut the cake into three equal-sized pieces. With a pastry brush, brush the top of each piece with orange-flavoured liqueur or Amaretto.
2 Line a 1 kg (2 lb), 23 x 10 x 7.5 cm (9 x 4 x 3 inch), loaf tin with baking parchment. Put one layer of cake, liqueur side up, in the tin and spread with half of the cream filling. Top with a second cake layer, liqueur side up, and spread with the remaining cream. Top with the last layer of cake, liqueur side down. Cover and refrigerate for at least 1 hour. (It can stay in the fridge overnight, if necessary.)
3 Unmould the cake on to a serving plate and brush the glaze on the top. Store in the fridge until needed.

Note

Rosettes of Orange Cream (page 150) can be piped on top to decorate the glazed cake.

Chocolate Ginger Roulade

CALORIE COUNT 110 KCAL FAT CONTENT 3G PER SLICE

I love this combination, but use any filling that suits your fancy: Raspberry Cream, Orange Cream or Cherry Cream (see page 150).

> one Chocolate Angel Sheet Cake (page 23)
> about ¹/₂ quantity Ginger Cream (page 154)
> 1 tablespoon finely grated high-cocoa-solid dark chocolate (see Note on page 24)

> Makes 12 slices

1 When the cake is cool, turn it out of its tin on to a clean tea towel and peel off the lining paper.
2 Spread the cake with the cream, leaving a 1 cm (¹/₂ inch) border around the edges. Starting with a long edge, carefully roll the cake, using the tea towel to help you along. Occasionally, the cake will crack, but it won't matter. Carefully transfer to a platter, and sprinkle on the grated chocolate. Store in the fridge until needed.

Cherry-Filled Chocolate Roulade

CALORIE COUNT 204 KCAL FAT CONTENT 5G PER SLICE

This cherry-filled variation is slathered with a dark, rich chocolate icing.

> one Chocolate Angel Sheet Cake (page 23)
> about ¹/₂ quantity Amaretti Cherry Mousse (page 49)
> Old-Fashioned Dark Chocolate Pudding or Spread (page 109)

> Makes 12 slices

1 When the cake is cool, turn it out of its tin on to a clean tea towel and peel off the lining paper.
2 Spread the cake with the mousse, leaving a 1 cm (¹/₂ inch) border around the edges. Starting with a long edge, carefully roll the cake, using the tea towel to help you along. Occasionally, the cake will crack, but it won't matter. Carefully transfer to a platter, and slather on the chocolate spread. Store in the fridge until needed.

The Prune Connection

A low-fat technique that has been doing the rounds for a few years now involves substituting prune purée for the fat in cake recipes. The first prune purée recipe to gain prominence was for a version of that squidgy, dark, fudgy miracle of chocolate-cake-making, the brownie. Now, in my view, a brownie containing prune purée instead of butter is not a brownie at all – it's an aberrant pruney thing – so for years I simply ignored the whole concept. Recently, however, a new product – 'Lighter Bake' – arrived on the supermarket shelves: a prune and apple purée meant to be used as a fat substitute in moist and chewy cakes and biscuits. It impelled me finally to try dried fruit purées in various baked goods. The following cake layers and the Prune and Ginger cake on page 31 are based on recipes developed by the 'Lighter Bake' people (Sunsweet), and I've had great success with them – I like them and all my tasters have enjoyed them. I've tested them all with 'Lighter Bake', Prune Purée (see page 149), and (my favourite) Hunza Apricot Purée (see page 146).

Cake Layers

CALORIE COUNT 808 KCAL FAT CONTENT 9G PER WHOLE LAYER

This recipe makes a lovely layer cake. It contains whole eggs (see page 10 for a discussion of eggs in low-fat cooking) but no other added fat. (Obviously, each serving of the cake contains only a fraction of a yolk.) Fill the cake with Hunza Apricot Purée (see page 146) and sprinkle the top with grated high-cocoa-solid dark chocolate or glaze the top with apricot jam (see page 154). Alternatively, you could fill the layers with ordinary Dried Apricot Purée (see page 148), or bottled high-fruit apricot spread, or Old-Fashioned Dark Chocolate Pudding or Spread (see page 109), or with any of the 'creams' (pages 150–154) that take your fancy.

> $4^{1}/_{2}$ tablespoons Lighter Bake, Prune Purée (see page 149) or Hunza Apricot Purée (page 146)
> 175 g (6 oz) caster sugar
> 3 eggs
> grated zest of 1 orange and 1 lemon
> 175 g (6 oz) self-raising flour, sifted

Makes 2 x 18 cm (7 inch) cake layers

1 Preheat the oven to 180°C, 350°F, Gas Mark 4. Line the base and sides of two 18 cm (7 inch) sandwich cake tins with baking parchment.
2 Whisk together the purée, sugar, eggs and zest until foamy, then fold in the flour. Divide the mixture between the two prepared tins. Bake in the oven for 12–15 minutes or until pale golden, and the sponges spring back when lightly touched. Turn out and leave to cool on wire racks.

Cornmeal Blueberry Cake

CALORIE COUNT 165 KCAL FAT CONTENT <1G PER SLICE

Although meringue is stirred and folded into the cooked polenta, the resulting cake is dense and squidgy rather than soufflé-like. Don't substitute fresh blueberries for dried – they are too wet. If you can't find the dried, use raisins instead. This cake makes a great brunch dessert. Serve in wedges with Blueberry Compote (see page 147) and Blueberry Cream (see page 150).

oil and water spray (page 10)
6 egg whites
pinch of cream of tartar
150 g (5 oz) caster sugar
550 ml (18 fl oz) water
pinch of salt
1 tablespoon natural vanilla extract
$1/4$ teaspoon ground cinnamon
175 g (6 oz) quick-cooking polenta
75 g ($2^1/_2$ oz) dried blueberries
150 g (5 oz) self-raising flour
1 teaspoon baking powder

Makes one 20 cm (8 inch) cake; 12 slices

1 Preheat the oven to 180°C, 350°F, Gas Mark 4. Spray a round 20 cm (8 inch) diameter, 5 cm (2 inches) deep, non-stick, loose-bottomed cake tin with oil and water.
2 Put the egg whites in a large bowl with the cream of tartar and beat with an electric mixer until they hold soft peaks. Beat in the sugar, a little at a time, until the whites hold firm peaks, are glossy, and the sugar is dissolved.
3 Put the water in a saucepan and bring almost to the boil. Add the salt, vanilla and cinnamon. Pour in the polenta in an even stream, whisking well all the time. Cook, stirring with a wooden spoon, until the mixture is smooth and thick, and pulls away from the sides of the pan. (This happens very quickly.)
4 Add the dried berries to the polenta, and stir in half of the meringue mixture to lighten it. When well blended, fold in the remaining meringue, the flour and baking powder.
5 Spoon the mixture into the prepared tin and bake in the oven for 50–55

minutes or until the top is dry and slightly cracked, and a cake tester inserted in the centre comes out clean. With a palette knife, loosen the cake all around, then remove the sides of the tin. Leave to cool on a wire rack.

Prune and Ginger Cake

CALORIE COUNT 144 KCAL FAT CONTENT 1G PER SLICE   (TRADITIONAL RECIPE CALORIE COUNT 242 KCAL FAT CONTENT 7G)

This makes a wonderfully moist, chewy, gingery cake. I like to serve it with Ginger Cream (see page 154). If you wish, you could give the top a marmalade glaze (see page 154).

oil and water spray (page 10)
200 g (7 oz) icing sugar
5 tablespoons Lighter Bake or Prune Purée (page 149)
2 large eggs, beaten
1 teaspoon natural vanilla extract
150 g (5 oz) plain flour
$1/2$ teaspoon baking powder
55 g ($1^3/_4$ oz) chopped crystallised ginger (use scissors)
grated zest of 2 lemons
3 tablespoons boiling water

Makes one 20 cm (8 inch) cake; 12 slices

1 Preheat the oven to 160°C, 325°F, Gas Mark 3. Spray a round 20 cm (8 inch) diameter, 5 cm (2 inches) deep, non-stick, loose-bottomed cake tin with oil and water.
2 Put the icing sugar and purée into a mixing bowl, and beat until smooth and well blended. Mix in the eggs and vanilla. Sift the flour and baking powder together over the mixture, and stir in. Stir in the crystallised ginger, lemon zest and boiling water.
3 Spread the mixture in the prepared tin and bake in the oven for 35–40 minutes or until a cake tested inserted in the centre of the cake comes out clean. Leave to cool in the tin for 10 minutes, then turn out on to a wire rack and leave to cool completely. Wrap, and store at room temperature until ready to serve.

Apricot-Filled Spice Crescents

CALORIE COUNT 125 KCAL   FAT CONTENT <0.5G PER SLICE

These spicy crescents are made with a basic soda bread dough. It is important not to overwork the dough or the resulting crescents will be tough. If you don't have (or don't like) ground cardamom, use a little ground mixed spice instead. This is a beautiful sweet bread for brunch or tea.

500 g (1 lb) self-raising flour, plus extra, as needed

$^1/_2$ orange and $^1/_2$ lemon

250 ml (8 fl oz) very low-fat fromage frais

200 ml (7 fl oz) skimmed milk

$^1/_2$ tablespoon natural vanilla extract

3 tablespoons runny honey

$^1/_4$ teaspoon ground cinnamon

$^1/_4$ teaspoon ground cardamom (see Note, opposite)

pinch of ground ginger

about 2 tablespoons Dried Apricot Purée (page 148)

Makes 2 loaves; approximately 8 slices each

1 Preheat the oven to 180°C, 350°F, Gas Mark 4.

2 Put the flour into a large mixing bowl, and grate the zest from the orange and lemon, holding the fruit over the bowl. With your hand, make a well in the centre of the flour.

3 Whisk together the fromage frais, milk, vanilla, honey and spices, and pour into the well.

4 With a wooden spoon, gradually stir the flour into the liquid. When it forms a rough, wet dough, flour your hands and knead the dough lightly and gently in the bowl.

5 Turn the dough out on to a lightly floured board, and knead quickly and lightly, turning the dough a few times and adding a dusting or two of flour, as needed, to form a smooth, soft, malleable dough.

6 Cut the dough into two equal pieces and roll each piece, *lightly* flouring the surface of the dough, and turning it as you roll, into a 15–18 cm (6–7 inch) circle or oval. Spread the apricot purée over the dough, leaving a margin all around the edge. Fold in the short sides (if you have rolled oval shapes), and roll from a long edge like a Swiss roll. Curve each into a crescent.

7 Put the crescents on to a floured baking sheet, well spaced apart (they will

expand as they bake and you don't want them to cook together). Bake in the oven for 35–45 minutes or until they are browned and baked through. Turn the crescents over for the last 10 minutes of cooking, so that they don't overbrown. They are done when a sharp knuckle rap on the bottom produces a hollow sound. Cool on a wire rack. Serve in slices.

Note

- Ground cardamom is available from many ethnic, speciality and wholefood shops. If you can't find it, buy green cardamom pods (available in virtually every supermarket), open the pods and grind the black seeds with a spice grinder or in a mortar and pestle.

- If you wish, omit the filling and form the dough into soda bread rounds instead. Prepare the recipe through step 5. The spices can be omitted (substitute a pinch of salt or whatever spice you like). Form the dough into two plump round loaves, place on a floured baking sheet and cut a shallow cross on the top of each. Bake as described in step 7. Also if you wish, you can substitute self-raising brown flour for half the white.

Sweet Potato Apricot Loaf

CALORIE COUNT 199 KCAL FAT CONTENT <1G PER SLICE

Orange-fleshed sweet potatoes and dried apricots give this loaf fantastic moistness, colour and flavour. The nutritional boost is rather fantastic as well; these are 'powerpack' foods. The cake keeps well, too, and improves in flavour over a period of days.

oil and water spray (page 10)

250 g (8 oz) ready-to-eat dried apricots, diced (use scissors)

250 ml (8 fl oz) orange juice

3 tablespoons red vermouth

150 g (5 oz) Granny Smith apples, peeled, cored and diced

175 g (6 oz) finely grated sweet orange-fleshed potatoes

300 g (10 oz) self-raising flour

1 teaspoon baking powder

pinch of salt

2 egg whites

pinch of cream of tartar

165 g ($5^1/2$ oz) soft brown sugar

Makes one 1.25–1.5 kg ($2^1/2$–3 lb) loaf; 12 slices

1 Preheat the oven to 160°C, 325°F, Gas Mark 3. Line a 1.25–1.5 kg ($2^1/2$–3 lb) non-stick loaf tin with greaseproof paper and spray with oil and water.

2 Put the apricots, orange juice, vermouth, apples and sweet potatoes into a saucepan. Bring to the boil, then remove from the heat and set aside. Sift the flour, baking powder and salt together into a bowl.

3 Whisk the egg whites with the cream of tartar until they hold soft peaks, then gradually whisk in the sugar, to make a stiff, glossy meringue.

4 Add the fruit mixture to the flour, beating well for 1–2 minutes. Fold in the meringue.

5 Scrape the mixture into the prepared tin, smooth the surface and bake in the oven for about 2 hours, covering loosely with foil for the last half hour or so that the loaf does not overbrown.

6 When the loaf is risen and golden brown, check that it is done by inserting a cake tester into the centre. When it comes out clean, the loaf is done. Cool in the tin on a wire rack for a few minutes, then loosen carefully all around the sides with a palette knife. Turn the loaf out on to the rack, peel off the greaseproof paper and leave to cool completely. To store, wrap in foil.

Beetroot Cake

CALORIE COUNT 225 KCAL FAT CONTENT <1G PER SLICE

Don't worry if the idea of beetroot makes you nervous; use grated carrot instead. However, beetroot produces an intensely red cake, absolutely beautiful on the plate and delicious on the palate. It would be a mistake not to try it at least.

oil and water spray (page 10)

175 g (6 oz) dried cranberries

250 ml (8 fl oz) cranberry juice

grated zest of 1 orange

150 g (5 oz) Granny Smith apples (about 2) or other tart
    eating apples, peeled, cored and finely diced

175 g (6 oz) finely grated beetroot

300 g (10 oz) self-raising flour

1 teaspoon baking powder

pinch of salt

2 egg whites

pinch of cream of tartar

165 g (5¹/₂ oz) soft brown sugar

Makes one 1 kg (2 lb) loaf; 12 slices

1 Preheat the oven to 160°C, 325°F, Gas Mark 3. Line a 1 kg (2 lb) non-stick loaf tin with greaseproof paper and spray with oil and water.

2 Place the cherries, cranberries, juice, zest, apples and beetroot in a saucepan. Bring to the boil, then remove from the heat and leave to cool. Sift the flour, baking powder and salt together into a bowl.

3 Put the egg whites and cream of tartar into another bowl, and whisk until they hold soft peaks. Gradually whisk in the sugar to make a stiff, glossy meringue.

4 Add the fruit mixture to the flour, beating well for 1–2 minutes, then fold in the meringue.

5 Scrape the mixture into the prepared tin, smooth the top and bake in the oven for about 2 hours, covering loosely with foil for the last half hour or so to prevent the loaf overbrowning.

6 When the loaf is risen and golden brown, check that it is done by inserting a cake tester or fine metal skewer into the centre. When it comes out clean, the loaf is done. Cool in the tin on a wire rack for a few minutes, then loosen carefully all around the sides with a palette knife. Turn the loaf out on to the rack, peel off the greaseproof paper and leave to cool completely.

Fruit Parsnip Loaf

CALORIE COUNT 220 KCAL FAT CONTENT <1G PER SLICE   (TRADITIONAL RECIPE CALORIE COUNT 394 KCAL FAT CONTENT 27G)

Like carrot, parsnip is naturally sweet, and perfect for cake baking. I first tasted parsnip cake at The Justin De Blank Café at the Barbican. It was quite rich with butter, but I knew it was an ideal candidate for low-fat tinkering.

oil and water spray (page 10)

250 g (8 oz) sultanas or raisins

250 ml (8 fl oz) orange juice

150 g (5 oz) Granny Smith apples, peeled, cored and diced

175 g (6 oz) finely grated parsnip (about 4 peeled parsnips)

300 g (10 oz) self-raising flour

1 teaspoon baking powder

pinch of salt

1 teaspoon ground cinnamon

3 teaspoons ground mixed spice

2 egg whites

pinch of cream of tartar

165 g (5^1/$_2$ oz) soft brown sugar

Makes one 1.25–1.5 kg (2^1/$_2$–3 lb) loaf; 12 slices

1 Preheat the oven to 160°C, 325°F, Gas Mark 3. Line a 1.25–1.5 kg (2^1/$_2$–3 lb) non-stick loaf tin with greaseproof paper and spray with oil and water.

2 Put the sultanas or raisins, orange juice, apples and parsnips into a saucepan. Bring to the boil, then remove from the heat and set aside. Sift the flour, baking powder, salt and spices together into a bowl.

3 Put the egg whites and cream of tartar into another bowl, and whisk until they hold soft peaks. Gradually whisk in the sugar to make a stiff, glossy meringue.

4 Add the fruit mixture to the flour, beating well for 1–2 minutes, then fold in the meringue.

5 Scrape the mixture into the prepared tin, smooth the top and bake in the oven for about 2 hours, covering loosely with foil for the last half hour or so to prevent the loaf overbrowning.

6 When the loaf is risen and golden brown, check that it is done by inserting a cake tester or fine metal skewer into the centre. When it comes out clean, the loaf is done. Cool in the tin on a wire rack for a few minutes, then loosen carefully all around the sides with a palette knife. Turn the loaf out on to the rack, peel off the greaseproof paper, and leave to cool completely.

CHAPTER 2

CHEESECAKES

I've been thinking about a low-fat cheesecake for years, but have been reluctant actually to tackle this sacred culinary icon; somehow I felt that there were some things that just shouldn't be fiddled with.

I grew up on New York deli food, so New York deli cheesecake – the ultimate of ultimates – has been part of my gastronomic consciousness for as long as I can remember. In the eighties I researched a book on New York's Jewish delis, and I was taken under the wing of the late Leo Steiner of the fabled Carnegie Deli. During that time I learned quite a bit about the rules governing real cheesecake. I never did get the recipe for the Carnegie's cheesecake – there are some questions you just don't ask – but I did learn that a *real* Jewish cheesecake has a crumb crust rather than a pastry one, *never* has a fruit topping, and is made with the richest, purest ingredients available.

The recipe I baked at home, and eventually put into my deli book, was from Lindy's, the legendary Broadway restaurant, purveyor of cheesecakes and strudels, immortalised by Frank Loesser in *Guys and Dolls*. It contained 1.25 kg (2½ lb) full-fat cream cheese (80 per cent fat), 5 eggs plus extra yolks, and a good slurp of double cream. The crumb crust contained plenty of butter and crumbed Graham Crackers (similar to Digestive biscuits). The cake was outrageously rich, creamy, suave and mouth-filling, and it was always served in *large* wedges. One slice (one twelfth) of a large cake contained 600 Calories and 47 grams of fat. Jane and Michael Stern described it in *Good Food* in 1983 as 'The richest dessert in history; pure edible ivory, like some new element on the atomic chart – perhaps a fusion of lead and satin', so you can see why I felt that trying to tame this excess would be like trying to make Marlene Dietrich sing soprano, or Mae West teach Sunday school!

However, years of cheesecake deprivation were very hard. Oh, how I hankered for just one slice. And my publisher, Judy Piatkus, hankered as well. Every time I saw her, she cast soulful glances in my direction, wondering when I would get around to conquering the cheesecake, and would leave subtle little messages with my editor about the possibility of including cheesecake in our next book. So I did it. No kidding, I really did. The first time I left some of my New Wave Deli Cheesecake in the fridge for my husband to taste, he accused me of cheating. It tasted like the real thing; how *could* it be low-fat? Well it is, and you can make it yourself out of easily obtained ingredients. How I *love* my work!

CHEESECAKE STRATEGY

There are a few pitfalls in classic cheesecake production. I'm going to try to talk you through the potential problems, so that your cheesecakes will be perfect every time.

Baking Tins

You'll need good springform tins for the cheesecakes in this chapter: a 25 cm (10 inch) tin for the first three recipes, and a 23 cm (9 inch) tin for the chocolate and raspberry recipe. A cheap, poorly made springform tin won't do; the liquid cheesecake mixture will flood through the cracks and make an almighty mess. Buy one of good quality (available by mail order, if necessary; see page 156), and make sure that the ring is snapped on properly. Just in case, always stand the tin on a baking tray before pouring in the cheesecake mixture.

Greasing and Sealing the Tin

Grease the tin by spraying it inside with oil and water (see page 10) before spreading the crumb crust mixture (see page 140) over the bottom and up the sides. (During baking, the crust helps to seal the edges and prevent leaks.)

Oven Temperature

This is a tricky one. The original recipe calls for 12 minutes of initial baking at 250°C, 500°F, Gas Mark 10, followed by 45 minutes at 100°C, 200°F, Gas Mark ¹/₄. These cakes are woefully prone to cracking, and the initial high heat is necessary to set the mixture. My cheesecake is excessively low in fat, so it is even more fragile than the original. The initial high heat is therefore particularly important, and 12 minutes is not long enough. Moreover, most home ovens don't go up to 250°C, 500°F, Gas Mark 10, and every oven is different. My assistant, Sandie, and I made dozens of cheesecakes in several different ovens and each oven gave slightly different results, so you must find what's right for yours. Here are the guidelines:

- If the initial baking is too cool and too short, the cake will be pale on top, and will crack dramatically. It is virtually impossible to produce a cheesecake of this type with no cracks at all, but when it looks like the Grand Canyon I draw the line.
- If the initial high-heat baking is too long, the finished cake will be dark on top and charred and crisp in places.

A nice golden brown is what we aim for.

Either way, too light and cracked or too dark and crisp, the cake will be delicious. In the first instance, the cake will be creamy and a bit loose; in the second, it will be drier and quite set, but yum-yum all the same.

The New York Deli Cheesecake recipe that follows gives a basic temperature and time for the initial baking that is my best estimate based on my multi-testing experience. If your cake is too dark and semi-charred on top, reduce the initial high-temperature cooking time somewhat; if it is too pale and disastrously cracked in several long trenches right through the cake, increase the time. The first cheesecake you bake will be a test run, and the cake will still be wonderful to eat even if the results are less than perfect. If cracked badly, slice it in the kitchen, working around the cracks, or hide it by covering it with a fruit topping, such as the one on page 43. Your cheesecake will no longer be ethnically pure, but since we've already thrown out the traditional butterfat, why worry?

Resting and Cooling Time

Follow the directions for leaving the oven door closed, cooling, loosening and chilling carefully, because all of these steps help keep the cake intact.

Is a cheesecake worth all this palaver, you might ask? You bet it is. As far as I'm concerned, a world containing a healthier yet gorgeous cheesecake is a happier place to live.

New York Deli CheeseCake

CALORIE COUNT 248 KCAL FAT CONTENT 4G PER SERVING   (TRADITIONAL RECIPE CALORIE COUNT 600 KCAL FAT CONTENT 47G)

This has an impossibly rich, voluptuous quality that makes it taste wickedly fattening. This cake and those that follow keep very well (at least a week) and they seem to improve as they age. Make sure that the soft cheese you choose contains less than 7 per cent fat, and plan ahead so that all your ingredients are at room temperature. Read through the trouble-shooting notes on page 38-9 before you begin.

1 Amaretti-Flavoured Crumb Crust (page 140) made in a 25 cm (10 inch) springform tin.

5 x 200 g (7 oz) tub light soft cheese (at room temperature)

3 tablespoons plain flour

325 g (11 oz) caster sugar

3 tablespoons natural vanilla extract

3 tablespoons fresh lemon juice

8 egg whites (at room temperature)

3 tablespoons very low-fat fromage frais (at room temperature)

Serves 14-16

1 Preheat the oven to 240°C, 475°F, Gas Mark 8.
2 Cream the cheese with an electric mixer until soft and fluffy. Beat in the flour, then beat in the sugar, a little at a time. Gradually add in the vanilla extract, lemon juice, egg whites and fromage frais, beating very well each time.
3 Pour in the cheese mixture. Bake in the oven for 20 minutes, then turn the oven down to 100°C, 200°F, Gas Mark 1/4 and bake for a further 40 minutes.
4 Turn the oven off and leave the cake in the oven for 1 hour, then open the oven door and, without removing the tin from the oven, *very gently* loosen the cake from the tin all around the edge with a palette knife. Leave the cheesecake in the open oven for 30 minutes.
5 Remove the tin from the oven and let it stand on a wire rack for at least 1 hour, until no longer warm.
6 Refrigerate the cake in the tin for at least 5 hours before removing the side of the tin. *This is very important; the cake may collapse if the 5-hour period is cut short.*

New York Italian Ricotta Cheesecake

CALORIE COUNT 274 KCAL FAT CONTENT 6G PER SERVING   (TRADITIONAL RECIPE CALORIE COUNT 512 KCAL FAT CONTENT 34G)

This New York cheesecake has an Italian rather than a Jewish heritage. I learned the original from my old friend Anne Masselli (wife of Paul Masselli, the sausage king). It was her mother's recipe, and is much less prone to cracking than the previous two. It doesn't have the dense, velvety richness of the Jewish version, and is perfect if you want to serve a dramatic, fruit-topped cake for dessert.

1 Amaretti-Flavoured Crumb Crust (page 140) made in a 25 cm (10 inch) springform tin

Fruit topping and glaze (optional), see below

Filling

2 x 200 g (7 oz) tub light soft cheese

2 x 250 g (8 oz) tub ricotta

500 g 1(1 lb) tub very low-fat fromage frais

300 g (10 oz) caster sugar

1 whole egg

4 egg whites

5 teaspoons natural vanilla extract

5 teaspoons fresh lemon juice

3 tablespoons plain flour

3 tablespoons cornflour

oil and water spray (page 10)

Serves 14–16

1 Preheat the oven to 180°C, 350°F, Gas Mark 4.
2 Put the light soft cheese, ricotta and fromage frais in a bowl and beat together with an electric mixer. Gradually beat in the sugar, followed by the remaining ingredients a little at a time, until everything is very well combined.
3 Pour in the cheese mixture. Bake in the oven for 1 hour, then turn off the oven (do not open the oven door) and leave the cake in the oven for 1 hour longer.
4 Open the oven door and, without removing the tin from the oven, very gently loosen the cake from the tin all around the edge with a palette knife. Leave the cheesecake in the open oven for 30 minutes.

5 Remove the cake from the oven and let it stand on a wire rack until cool. Refrigerate overnight.
6 Next day, remove the side of the springform tin. Top the cheesecake with fruit and glaze if you wish (see below).

Fruit Topping and Glaze for Cheesecakes

1 Heat some strawberry conserve in a saucepan over a low heat until melted. Cool until lukewarm.
2 Meanwhile, hull some beautiful strawberries and arrange them, pointed ends up, on the cooled cheesecake, covering the surface completely. Brush on the melted conserve and refrigerate until needed.

Variations

Use blueberries and melted blueberry conserve, or raspberries with melted raspberry conserve, or peaches or nectarines with peach conserve. Alternatively, use a combination: blueberries on one quarter of the cheesecake, raspberries on a second quarter, strawberries on a third, and peaches on the final quarter.

Chocolate and Raspberry Cheesecake

CALORIE COUNT 303 KCAL FAT CONTENT 6G PER SERVING   (TRADITIONAL RECIPE CALORIE COUNT 436 KCAL FAT CONTENT 30G)

This is not an ethnic cheesecake at all. It's from Middle America and is based on an extremely high-fat recipe I admired in a magazine, and thought – in my usual arrogant way – that I could easily de-fat. This is a slightly tart, multi-layered cheesecake with chocolate on the bottom, raspberry on the top.

1 Chocolate Amaretti-Flavoured Crumb Crust (page 140) made in a 23 cm (9 inch) springform tin

fresh raspberries, to serve

Filling

250 g (8 oz) frozen raspberries, thawed and thoroughly drained

1 teaspoon caster sugar

90 g (3 oz) high-cocoa-solid dark chocolate

3 x 200 g (7 oz) tub light soft cheese

405 g (13 oz) can sweetened condensed skimmed milk

5 egg whites

1 teaspoon natural vanilla extract

oil and water spray

Serves 10–12

1 Preheat the oven to 180°C, 350°F, Gas Mark 4.
2 Purée the raspberries in a blender or food processor, then rub through a nylon sieve to eliminate the seeds. Stir in the sugar.
3 Melt the chocolate in a heatproof bowl over a pan of simmering water, then leave to cool slightly.
4 Put the light soft cheese and condensed milk in a bowl and beat with an electric mixer until very smooth, creamy and fluffy.
5 Add the egg whites and vanilla, a little at a time, beating until very well combined between each addition. Pour half the mixture into a jug and stir in the melted chocolate. (Use a rubber spatula to get every last bit of chocolate out of the bowl.) Mix well. Pour in the chocolate mixture. Gently stir the raspberry purée into the remaining mixture, and pour it over the chocolate mixture with a gentle swirling motion.

6 Bake in the oven for 50–60 minutes or until the edge of the cheesecake is firm, and the centre is ever-so-slightly wobbly when shaken. Cool in the tin on a wire rack for 15 minutes, then loosen the cake from the tin around the edge. Let it stand until thoroughly cooled, then cover and refrigerate for at least 4 hours before removing the side of the tin. Serve with raspberries.

Variation

The cake can be made with whole raspberries rather than a purée, as long as you don't mind the seeds. The raspberry flavour will be a little more pronounced, and the whole berries will look dramatic in each slice. Drain the berries, but leave them unpuréed, and toss with 1 teaspoon sugar. Mix them gently into the second half of the mixture (step 5), and continue as above.

'Wildly excessive, very wet, intensely sweet, heavy, thickly studded with fruit.'

Cheesecake description: Seymour Britchky,

The Restaurants of New York

Chocolate and Orange Cheesecake

CALORIE COUNT 269 KCAL FAT CONTENT 5G PER SERVING

This is a seductive variation on the classic. The chocolate is a subtle whisper between cake and crust.

60 g (2 oz) high-cocoa-solid dark chocolate

1 Chocolate Amaretti-Flavoured Crumb Crust (page 140)
   made in a 25 cm (10 inch) springform tin

Filling

5 x 200 g (7 oz) tub light soft cheese (at room temperature)

3 tablespoons plain flour

325 g (11 oz) caster sugar

3 tablespoons natural vanilla extract

3 tablespoons fresh orange juice

grated zest of 1/2 orange

8 egg whites (at room temperature)

3 tablespoons very low-fat fromage frais (at room temperature)

oil and water spray (page 10)

Serves 14–16

1 Preheat the oven to 240°C, 475°F, Gas Mark 9. Melt the chocolate in a heatproof bowl over a pan of simmering water.

2 Spread the melted chocolate over the crumb base in the tin and leave to set.

3 Cream the cheese until soft and fluffy. Beat in the flour, then beat in the sugar, a little at a time. Gradually beat in the vanilla extract, orange juice, orange zest, egg whites and fromage frais, beating very well between each addition.

4 Pour in the cheese mixture. Bake in the oven for 20 minutes, then turn the oven down to 100°C, 200°F, Gas Mark 1/4 and bake for a further 40 minutes.

5 Turn the oven off and leave the cake in the oven for 1 hour, then open the door and, without removing the tin from the oven, *very gently* loosen the cake from the tin all around the edge with a palette knife. Leave the cheesecake in the open oven for 30 minutes.

6 Remove the tin from the oven and let it stand on a wire rack for at least 1 hour, until no longer warm.

7 Refrigerate the cake in the tin for at least 5 hours before removing the side of the tin. *This is very important; the cake may collapse if the 5-hour period is cut short.*

Yogurt and Ricotta Cream Berry Tart with Apricot Glaze

CALORIE COUNT 325 KCAL FAT CONTENT 8G PER SERVING   (TRADITIONAL RECIPE CALORIE COUNT 398 KCAL FAT CONTENT 20G)

This stunning fruit tart has an amaretti crumb base, a filling of silky drained ricotta and yogurt sweetened with honey and orange marmalade, and a vivid topping of berries under an apricot glaze. Peaches or nectarines can be used instead of the berries; in fact slices of mango (arranged in a pinwheel pattern) would be quite effective as well. The flavour of the marmalade and glaze can be changed according to the fruit used.

1 kg (2 lb) carton very low-fat natural yogurt

2 x 250 g (8 oz) carton ricotta

2 teaspoons natural vanilla extract

about 2 tablespoons runny honey

about 1 tablespoon orange marmalade

1 Amaretti-Flavoured Crumb Crust (page 140) made in a 25 cm (10 inch) pie tin

mixed fresh berries (e.g. blueberries, quartered strawberries, raspberries), or chosen fruit (see above)

2 tablespoons apricot conserve, melted

Serves 8

1 Line a sieve with a clean, dampened and wrung out blue J-cloth (pink leaks dye) or piece of butter muslin, and place over a deep bowl. Pour the yogurt into the sieve, fold over the cloth, and leave to drain overnight (or for at least 8 hours). Pour off the liquid occasionally.

2 Do the same with the ricotta, using a smaller sieve.

3 Next day, or when drained, put both the yogurt and the ricotta into a food processor with the vanilla, honey and marmalade. (The exact amount of sweetener needed depends on the tanginess of the yogurt and your taste.) Process until silky smooth.

4 Smooth the mixture into the crumb crust in the tin, and arrange the fruit on top in a beautiful pattern. Brush with the melted apricot conserve and refrigerate until needed.

Pineapple Cheese Pie

CALORIE COUNT 335 KCAL FAT CONTENT <6G PER SERVING

Another uncooked fruit and creamy-cheese tart, this one includes crushed pineapple and a touch of rum. To reduce the fat content even further, replace the ricotta with additional quark.

> 1 Amaretti-Flavoured Crumb Crust (page 140) made in a 25 cm (10 inch) pie tin

Filling
> 2 x 425 g (14 oz) can crushed pineapple in natural juice
>
> 2 x 250 g (8 oz) carton quark
>
> 1½ x 250 g (8 oz) carton ricotta
>
> 1 teaspoon natural vanilla extract
>
> 1 tablespoon dark rum
>
> pineapple conserve, pineapple and ginger conserve or orange marmalade, to taste
>
> 1–2 tablespoons crushed amaretti and Grape Nut crumbs

Serves 8

1 Drain the pineapple in a nylon sieve set over a bowl. Press down on the pineapple pulp to extract as much juice as possible. (Save the juice for another use.)
2 Put *half* the pineapple, and all of the quark, ricotta, vanilla and rum in a food processor, and process until very smooth and fluffy. Add conserve or marmalade to taste, and process until blended.
3 Tip the mixture into a bowl and gently fold in the remaining pineapple with a rubber spatula.
4 Line a sieve with a clean, dampened blue J-cloth (pink leaks dye) or piece of butter muslin, and place over a deep bowl. Scrape the cheese mixture into the sieve, refrigerate and allow to drain for 1–2 hours.
5 When the pineapple-cheese is firm and well drained, swirl and spread it into the crumb crust in the pie tin. Sprinkle the top evenly with the amaretti and Grape Nuts mixture, cover and chill overnight.

Right: Killer Chocolate Chestnut Layer Cake (page 112)

Amaretti Cherry Cheesecake Mousse

CALORIE COUNT 301 KCAL FAT CONTENT 8G PER SERVING

Deconstructed cheesecake: creamy almond-scented mousse in a goblet with a crunchy biscuit in place of a crust. The mixture could also be rolled in crêpes (page 85), swirled into a meringue pie shell (page 66) or spread between angel cake layers (page 22).

3 tablespoons sultanas
75 g (2¹/₂ oz) package dried cherries
1 teaspoon natural vanilla extract
1 teaspoon natural almond extract
4 tablespoons Amaretto di Saronno liqueur
125 ml (4 fl oz) water
250 g (8 oz) carton ricotta
250 g (8 oz) carton quark
¹/₂–1 tablespoon cherry conserve
4 Almond Biscuits (page 142), halved

Serves 4

1 Put the sultanas, cherries, vanilla and almond extracts, Amaretto and water in a small frying pan. Simmer until the fruit is plump and the liquid almost gone. Remove from the heat and leave to cool.
2 Spoon half the cooled mixture into a food processor and add the ricotta, quark and about 1 teaspoon of the cherry conserve. Process for a few seconds, then taste and add more conserve as required. Process again until the mixture is smooth and fluffy with flecks of almost-puréed fruit showing through.
3 Divide the mixture between four serving goblets, and top each with some of the reserved sultana and cherry mixture. Refrigerate for a few hours.
4 Push two almond biscuit halves halfway into each goblet at a jaunty angle. Serve at once.

Left: Yogurt and Ricotta Cream Berry Tart with Apricot Glaze (page 47)

Blueberry Rice Cream Pie

CALORIE COUNT 287 KCAL FAT CONTENT 7G PER SERVING

This makes an interesting family dessert: vanilla-scented rice crust, filled with deep purple blueberry compote and topped with a misty mauve cloud of ricotta cream.

1 Rice Pie Crust (page 141) made in a 28 cm (11 inch) non-stick flan dish

Blueberry Filling
500 g (1 lb) blueberries

1–3 tablespoons high fruit, no added sugar blueberry fruit spread

1 tablespoon cornflour

juice of $1/2$ lemon

1 teaspoon natural vanilla extract

Topping
2 x 250 g (8 oz) carton ricotta

250 g (8 oz) carton quark

1–2 tablespoons blueberry high fruit spread

1 tablespoon Cointreau or other orange-flavoured liqueur

1 teaspoon natural vanilla extract

Serves 8

1 Preheat the oven to 190°C, 375°F, Gas Mark 5. Combine the blueberry filling ingredients in a glass or ceramic baking dish, and bake, uncovered, in the oven for about 15 minutes, stirring occasionally, until the mixture is thickened and bubbling. Remove from the heat and leave to cool.
2 To make the cream topping, put all the ingredients in a food processor, and process until very well combined and fluffy.
3 Spread the blueberry filling over the rice base in the tin, leaving a 1 cm ($1/2$ inch) rim of rice showing. Swirl the cream topping over the blueberry filling, leaving a 5 mm ($1/4$ inch) rim of blueberry showing. Refrigerate until ready to serve.

Variation

Peach or Nectarine Rice Cream Pie

1 Substitute Peach (or nectarine) Compote (see page 146) for the blueberry filling.
2 Substitute peach conserve or preserves for the blueberry in the cream topping.

CHAPTER 3

TIRAMISUS, TRIFLES AND CREAMY DESSERTS

Tiramisù began as the quintessential Italian Mama's tonic for her poorly son, went on to become everyone's favourite bistro dessert, and now, I suspect, is totally *passé*. In its original form, it consists of sponge fingers dipped in coffee and liqueur, topped with mascarpone cheese (80 per cent fat), raw egg yolks, whisked raw egg whites and whipped cream. As far as I am concerned this is so *passé* it was never here! Oh, how I love reforming these butterfat monsters. Of course, the reborn creature must be incredibly delicious, or it's no earthly good at all.

For a simple tiramisù, sprinkle the sponge fingers with coffee and liqueur, and smother with ricotta or a combination of quark and ricotta, or low-fat soft cheese and ricotta mixed in a food processor with a touch of icing sugar. Sprinkle the top with icing sugar and/or cocoa powder, or with a little grated high-cocoa-solid dark chocolate.

The real fun of this sort of recipe, however, is in the variations; there are all sorts of possibilities. Two recipes for my most popular tiramisù variations appear in this chapter, plus several more suggestions for you to play with. You'll also find trifles, cream hearts, and other indulgent desserts. With ricotta standing in so well for whipped cream and crème fraîche, there is no need to axe creamy and indulgent desserts from your life.

Orange-Scented Tiramisù

CALORIE COUNT 211 KCAL FAT CONTENT 8G PER SERVING   (TRADITIONAL RECIPE CALORIE COUNT 602 KCAL FAT CONTENT 40G)

Leave out the Cointreau if this is to be served to children.

approximately 13–14 sponge fingers (see Note, below)
150 ml (5 fl oz) freshly squeezed orange juice
2 tablespoons Cointreau
1½ teaspoons natural vanilla extract
approximately 200 g (7 oz) ricotta and approximately 375 g (12 oz) quark
about 2 tablespoons orange marmalade
approximately 30 g (1 oz) high-cocoa-solid dark chocolate, grated

Serves 6–8

1 Line the bottom of a shallow, rectangular (30 x 18 cm/12 x 7 inch) or oval
   baking dish with one layer of sponge fingers. (You may have to break a few in
   half.) Stir together the orange juice, Cointreau and ½ teaspoon of the vanilla
   extract. Sprinkle this mixture over the sponge fingers, a tablespoon at a time.
2 Put the ricotta, marmalade and remaining vanilla in a food processor and
   process until smooth and fluffy, tasting as you go, and adding more
   marmalade if needed. Spread this mixture over the sponge fingers.
3 Sprinkle the top evenly with grated chocolate and chill until required.

Variations

• Cherries macerated in Cointreau, vanilla and a touch of orange juice spread on
  the sponge fingers, cherry conserve to flavour the 'cream', sifted icing sugar
  and low-fat unsweetened cocoa power sprinkled on top.
• Raspberries and strawberries macerated in Cointreau and orange juice spread
  on the sponge fingers, Chocolate Ricotta Mousse (see page 116) on top, and
  15 g (½ oz) high-cocoa-solid dark chocolate, grated and sprinkled on top.
• Amaretti Cherry Cheesecake Mousse (see page 49) spread on the sponge
  fingers (soak them first with Amaretto, orange juice and vanilla) topped with
  crushed amaretti biscuits.

Note

If you wish, add a layer of orange segments. Sponge fingers are made with
whole eggs, but no additional fat. If you want to reduce the fat even further,
substitute fingers of Angel Sheet Cake (see page 22) for the sponge fingers.

Chocolate Tiramisù

CALORIE COUNT 217 KCAL FAT CONTENT 6G PER SERVING

In this tiramisù variation (and the one described on
page 51), good decaffeinated can be used instead of
strong coffee.

15–16 sponge fingers
150 ml (5 fl oz) strong black coffee
1 tablespoon Amaretto di Saronno or Tia Maria
1 tablespoon dark rum
375 g (12 oz) each of ricotta and quark
$6^1/_2$ tablespoons icing sugar
$3^1/_2$ tablespoons low-fat unsweetened cocoa powder
$1^1/_2$ teaspoons natural vanilla extract
15 g ($^1/_2$ oz) high-cocoa-solid dark chocolate, melted and
    cooled slightly

Serves 6–8

1 Line the bottom of a shallow, rectangular (30 x 18 cm/12 x 7 inch) or oval
baking dish with one layer of sponge fingers. (You may have to break a few in
half.) Stir together the coffee, liqueur and rum. Sprinkle this mixture over the
sponge fingers, 1 tablespoon at a time.
2 Put the ricotta and quark, 6 tablespoons icing sugar, 2 tablespoons cocoa, 1
teaspoon vanilla and the melted chocolate into a food processor, and process
until smooth and fluffy. Spread this mixture smoothly over the sponge fingers.
3 Sift together the remaining cocoa and icing sugar, and sprinkle evenly over the
surface of the pudding. Cover and chill until required.

Chocolate and Raspberry Trifle

CALORIE COUNT 209 KCAL FAT CONTENT 6G PER SERVING

Anything goes with this trifle. Prepare individual ones in beautiful balloon goblets, or make a statement with an enormous one in a footed glass vessel. Mix and match the layers as you wish. This helter-skelter mixture makes joyous eating.

1 quantity Hot Chocolate Fudge Sauce (page 118), cooled
2 x 250 g (8 oz) carton ricotta
1 teaspoon natural vanilla extract
$^1/_2$ tablespoon high-fruit no-added-sugar raspberry spread
$^1/_4$–$^1/_2$ Chocolate Angel Cake (page 21), cubed
1 quantity Raspberry Coulis (page 144)
fresh raspberries
1 pair amaretti biscuits, crushed
grated high-cocoa-solid dark chocolate

Serves 10–12

1 Put half the chocolate fudge sauce in a food processor with half the ricotta, and process until smooth. Process the remaining ricotta with the vanilla and raspberry spread.
2 Put the cubes of angel cake into serving goblets. Spoon over some chocolate fudge sauce, and then a few tablespoons of raspberry coulis and some fresh raspberries. Top with some of the chocolate and ricotta mixture, and some of the vanilla and ricotta, then sprinkle on some amaretti crumbs and grated chocolate.

Variation

Orange-Scented trifle

Use cubes of Vanilla Angel Cake instead of chocolate, process the ricotta with 1 tablespoon orange marmalade and 1 teaspoon vanilla instead of chocolate fudge sauce, and omit the raspberry coulis. Sprinkle a mixture of orange juice, Cointreau and vanilla extract over the cake cubes first. If you have no angel cake to hand use broken sponge fingers, and add a layer of orange segments macerated in orange juice and Cointreau.

Instant Berry Trifles

CALORIE COUNT 228 KCAL FAT CONTENT 6G PER SERVING

From my *Quick After-Work Low-Fat Cookbook*, this trifle can be thrown together in moments (if your fridge, freezer and pantry are well stocked), yet it radiates pizzazz.

1 trifle sponge

a few tablespoons Raspberry Coulis (page 144)

2 – 3 tablespoons ricotta

about 1 teaspoon blueberry or cherry conserve

1 teaspoon natural vanilla extract

several generous tablespoons raspberries and blueberries (fresh or thawed if frozen)

1 amaretti biscuit, crushed

Serves 1

1 Tear the sponge into pieces and drop them into the bottom of a large serving goblet or an individual glass dessert bowl. Spoon over some of the coulis, and stir gently to saturate the sponge with the raspberry sauce.
2 Put the ricotta in a food processor with the fruit conserve and vanilla extract, and process until combined.
3 Heap the berries on top of the sponge, and drizzle on a little more coulis. Dollop on the ricotta, and sprinkle on the amaretti crumbs. Serve at once.

'One of those musty, fragrant, deep-ribbed cantaloups, chilled to the heart now in all their pink-flesh taste and ripeness... or a bowl of those red raspberries, most luscious and most rich'

Thomas Wolfe; *Of Time and the River*

Coeurs a La Creme

Coeur à la crème is a dramatic, creamy dessert; essentially a cream cheese mousse drained overnight in a perforated heart-shaped mould. If you don't have such a mould (see page 156 for stockists), use a sieve or colander instead. Although not heart-shaped, the dessert will taste just as nice. A coeur à la crème surrounded by a well-matched fruit salad makes a beautiful and delicious end to a meal. An exotic one follows, and then a lovely orange version. Using the ideas in the cream topping section (pages 150–54), and the fruit desserts chapter (see page 69), you can produce any number of coeur à la crème variations.

Ginger Lime and Cardamom Coeur a La Creme

CALORIE COUNT 137 KCAL FAT CONTENT 7G PER SERVING

2 tablespoons green cardamom pods
juice of 1 lime and 1 orange
grated zest of 1 lime
2.5 cm (1 inch) piece fresh root ginger, peeled and crushed
250 ml (8 fl oz) water
2 x 250 g (8 oz) carton ricotta
about 1 tablespoon lime shred marmalade or ginger
    conserve
Exotic Fruit Salad, to serve (see below)
torn mint leaves, to decorate

Serves 6–8

1 Lightly crush the cardamom pods and put into a small frying pan with the lime juice, orange juice, lime zest and ginger. Stir in the water, then bring to the boil and boil for about 10 minutes to reduce to a sticky syrup. Push through a sieve, pressing down on the solids, and leave to cool.
2 Put the ricotta in a food processor with the cooled syrup and the marmalade. Process until fluffy, then taste, and process in a little more marmalade if necessary.
3 Line a large 600 ml (1 pint) coeur à la crème mould or nylon sieve with a damp blue J-cloth (pink leaks dye) or piece of butter muslin. Place over a bowl and scrape in the ricotta mixture. Flip the ends of the cloth over to cover, and leave to drain in the refrigerator overnight.
4 Unmould on to a pretty plate, surround with fruit salad, and decorate with mint leaves.

Exotic Fruit Salad

Combine cubed papaya, melon, pineapple and blood oranges with sliced kiwi and star fruit. Squeeze in some blood orange juice and a dash or two of natural vanilla extract, Crème de Pêche and Cointreau. (If blood oranges are not available, use ordinary ones.) Allow to macerate for an hour or so before serving.

Orange Coeur a La Creme with Orange Salad

CALORIE COUNT 141 KCAL FAT CONTENT 7G PER SERVING

2 x 250 g (8 oz) carton ricotta
about 2 tablespoons orange marmalade
grated zest of $1/2$ large orange
$1^1/2$ teaspoons natural vanilla extract
Orange Salad, to serve (see below)

Serves 6–8

1 Put the ricotta and 1 tablespoon of the marmalade in a food processor, and grate the zest from the orange, holding the fruit over the ricotta. Add the vanilla and process until well combined and fluffy. Taste, then add more marmalade as needed.
2 Scrape the ricotta into a large lined mould or sieve and leave to drain as described in step 3 of the previous recipe.
3 Unmould on to a pretty plate, surround with the orange salad, and serve.

Orange Salad

1 Peel several seedless oranges and cut off all the bitter white pith. (If blood oranges are available, use 1–2 of them as well.) Cut the segments of fruit out from between the membranes (do this over a bowl to catch the juice), and place in the bowl.
2 Squeeze in a little more orange juice and scatter on some slivered zest. Stir in some vanilla (about $1/2$ teaspoon) and a dash or two of Cointreau, and leave to macerate until needed.

CHAPTER 4

MERINGUES

Cooking is the ultimate human ingenuity, the most intriguing blend of art and science. Consider the egg: its parts separated or together, in or out of its shell, it provides endless hours of happy play for the obsessive cook. From its humble origin (a chicken), it is brought to awe-inspiring heights of gastronomic play: soufflés, sabayons, emulsion sauces (Hollandaise et al), or it can be soft-boiled, hard-boiled, made into an omelette, scrambled, poached, coddled. . . Is there any other foodstuff that can be so endlessly permutated? Really, eggs are almost science fictional in their changeability and malleability.

As a low-fat cook discoursing on desserts, my interest right now is in meringue. When the whites of eggs are separated from the yolks and strenuously whisked with sugar, they magically thicken, increase in volume and take on a firm, glossy, marshmallow-cream texture that is quite astonishing when you consider the nature and appearance of the original, unbeaten white. At one time, this meringue was used raw, as a matter of course, to lighten all sorts of creamy mousses, but now fear of *Salmonellae* bacteria forbids this. To practise safe meringue technique for mousses and such, the whites must be cooked to a temperature of 60°C (140°F), and kept at that temperature for 3$^1/_2$ minutes. This involves the use of an instant-read or sugar thermometer, and constant beating (for 10 minutes all told) in a *bain-marie*.

For baked meringues, however, once the egg whites are whisked with sugar, they are simply bunged in the oven and left to set and dry out right through.

Meringue Strategy

Here are the guidelines for successful meringue making:

1 Plan ahead, and take the eggs out of the fridge several hours before you plan to use them. Cold egg whites will not whisk to their potential full volume. If you forget, warm the eggs, in their shells, in a bowl of warm water before you begin (or see page 21).

2 Separate the eggs carefully. Crack each egg open over a small clean bowl and shift the yolk from one eggshell half to the other, letting the white drip into the bowl. Tip the white into a second, larger bowl. Repeat this with all the eggs, using a clean small bowl each time. Why a clean bowl each time? First of all, if you are unlucky enough to get a bad egg (it happens) you don't want it contaminating the rest. Second, if you break the yolk as you tip it from one egg half to the other, and some of it gets into the white, you must put that one aside. The tiniest speck of yolk in the whites will prevent them from whisking into meringue. If some yolk does get into your whites, try to fish it out with the tip of a teaspoon, never the egg shell – after all, we all know exactly where that shell has been (under a chicken's bum).

3 Use an electric mixer and a large bowl to whisk the whites. All utensils must be spotlessly clean. The slightest speck of grease will prevent the whites from whisking into meringue.

4 The old-fashioned way to whisk egg whites into meringue is in a large, unlined copper bowl with a balloon whisk. A chemical reaction takes place between the copper and the whites which strengthens and stabilises them. However, you will achieve excellent results with a glass bowl and electric beaters if you add a pinch of cream of tartar to the whites early on, thus providing a similar chemical reaction.

5 Add the sugar to the whites slowly, making sure that it is thoroughly dissolved, or the baked meringues will 'weep' syrupy drops as they bake. Rub a speck of the beaten meringue between your fingers; if it feels grainy, the sugar has not completely dissolved.

What on earth to do with all those left-over yolks?

1 Feed them (cooked) to your dog. Dogs metabolise cholesterol differently from humans; the yolks will make your dog's coat shine.

2 Find a copy of Anita Guyton's excellent book *A Woman's Book of Natural Beauty* (Thorsons) and learn to make a hair conditioner from egg yolks. (Just don't turn on the hair dryer!)

3 Tempera painting was popular during the Middle Ages and during the early Italian Renaissance, and egg yolk mixed with pigment is the medium used for tempera painting. *The Artist's Manual* (Macdonald, 1980) will tell you all you need to know about turning your egg yolks into this classic preparation. Egg tempera paintings do not yellow and darken with age, as do oil paintings, and the colour dries much truer to the original pigment. According to *The Artist's Manual*, 'A work in tempera, painted on to a firm surface, will retain the freshness of its original colours, as many of the great paintings of the Middle Ages have done.'

Meringue Layer Torte

CALORIE COUNT 567 KCAL FAT CONTENT 1G PER WHOLE LAYER

If you are a dab hand with a piping bag, make these three layers and stack them with alternate fillings in between for an extraordinarily elegant celebration dessert. Possible filling ideas: Chocolate Chestnut Filling (see page 116) and Raspberry Cream (see page 150) – top with raspberries macerated in Framboise; Orange Cream (see page 150) and Chocolate Ricotta Mousse (see page 116) – top with strawberries macerated in a touch of Cointreau; Amaretti Cherry Cheesecake Mousse (see page 49) in both layers topped with stoned, halved cherries macerated in Amaretto di Saronno

5 egg whites (at room temperature)
pinch of cream of tartar
200 g (7 oz) caster sugar
1 teaspoon natural vanilla extract
filling and topping of your choice (see above)

Makes 3 layers

1 Preheat the oven to 120°C, 225°F, Gas Mark ¼.
2 Beat the egg whites with the cream of tartar in a large bowl with a hand-held electric mixer until foamy. Increase the speed of the mixer and continue beating as you add the sugar, 1–2 tablespoons at a time, until the whites are shiny and stiff and hold firm peaks. Fold in the vanilla.
3 Line three baking sheets with baking parchment and trace a 20 cm (8 inch) circle on each. Turn the paper over and pipe the meringue in concentric circles to fill each pencilled circle. Bake in the oven for 3 hours or until the meringues are beige, dry and crisp, and sound hollow when tapped lightly on the bottom. Leave in the turned-off oven for at least 3 hours until thoroughly cooled. (They may stay in overnight.)

Note

If you are *not* a dab hand with a piping bag, you can simply spread the meringue evenly to fill the circles.

Small Meringues

CALORIE COUNT 16 KCAL FAT CONTENT 0G PER MERINGUE

Shape these into little kisses, to sandwich together with various interesting fillings, or into slightly larger meringue tartlet cases. Fill the cases with Chocolate Chestnut Filling (see page 116), Old-Fashioned Dark Chocolate Pudding (see page 109), or berries with a yogurt or ricotta 'cream' (see pages 150–54). Serve the meringue kisses singly with Chocolate Sauce (page 117) drizzled all over them, or sandwiched together with Fig or Prune Filling (recipes follow), Dried Apricot Purée (see page 148), Amaretti Cherry Cheesecake Mousse (see page 49), one of the ricotta 'creams' or Old-Fashioned Dark Chocolate Pudding.

3 egg whites (at room temperature)
pinch each of cream of tartar and salt
150 g (5 oz) caster sugar
1 teaspoon natural vanilla extract

Makes approximately 40 small or 15 large meringues

1 Preheat the oven to 150°C, 300°F, Gas Mark 2. Line two large baking sheets with baking parchment.
2 Using a large, clean bowl and a hand-held electric mixer, beat the egg whites with the cream of tartar and salt until foamy. Increase the speed of the mixer and continue beating while adding the sugar, 1–2 tablespoons at a time, until the whites are shiny and stiff and hold firm peaks. Fold in the vanilla.
3 Drop teaspoons of the meringue on to the prepared baking sheets. Alternatively, use a tablespoon, space the meringues 2.5 cm (1 inch) apart, and make a shallow depression in the centre of each one with the back of the spoon. Bake in the oven for 45–60 minutes or until the meringues are beige, dry and crisp, and sound hollow when tapped lightly on the bottom.
4 Turn the oven off, and leave the meringues in the oven, with the door closed, for at least 3 hours. (They may stay in overnight.) Do not open the door until the time is up. Store the meringues in an airtight container.

Right: Fruit on Toast with orange and grapefruit segments and Winter Dried Fruit Compote (page 78)

Fillings for Meringue Kisses

I grew up with a marvellous biscuit called the Fig Newton. (I believe it is known as a Fig Roll in the UK – same biscuit, much more prosaic name.) The wonderful Fig Newton filling inspired me to develop a grown-up fig filling to sandwich between meringue biscuits. Prunes work well, too, although I know that some people find prunes too ridiculous for words. Please try the delicious mixture before you decide to snicker.

Fig Filling

CALORIE COUNT 40 KCAL FAT CONTENT <0.5G PER TABLESPOON

275 g (9 oz) package ready-to-eat dried figs
250 g (8 oz) carton quark
$^1/_4$ teaspoon natural vanilla extract
a few drops of maple syrup or runny honey (to taste)
a few drops of fresh lemon juice

Makes 300 ml ($^1/_2$ pint)

1 Stem and dice the figs and put them in a food processor with the quark and vanilla. Process until almost smooth.
2 Add a few drops of maple syrup or honey to taste (if any is needed at all) and a few drops of fresh lemon juice. Process until smooth. Taste and add more lemon juice and/or sweetener to taste, if necessary, then process once more to blend. Store in the refrigerator until needed.

Left: *Orange-Scented Trifle (page 53)*

Prune Filling

CALORIE COUNT 30 KCAL FAT CONTENT NEG PER TABLESPOON

275 g (9 oz) package ready-to-eat stoned prunes, diced
250 g (8 oz) carton quark
$^1/_4$ teaspoon natural vanilla extract
a few drops of maple syrup or runny honey (to taste)
a few drops of lemon juice
pinch of ground mace
pinch of ground cinnamon
pinch of ground allspice

Makes 300 ml ($^1/_2$ pint)

Put all the ingredients in a food processor and process until smooth. Taste, and process in a little more of any of the flavourings if you feel it needs it. Store in the refrigerator until needed

Rustic Meringue Pie

CALORIE COUNT 140 KCAL FAT CONTENT 2G PER SERVING   (TRADITIONAL RECIPE CALORIE COUNT 854 KCAL FAT CONTENT 60G)

A brittle meringue shell, filled with chocolate and bananas (see page 111), one of the ricotta 'creams' (see pages 150–54) and berries or cubed peaches, or Chocolate Ricotta Mousse (see page 116), or drained yogurt (see page 149) swirled with Hunza Apricot Purée (see page 146), makes a beautiful ending to a special meal. The meringue shell keeps for weeks in an airtight container, so you can make it well in advance. Here I've filled it with Orange Cream.

Rustic Meringue Pie Shell
4 egg whites (at room temperature)
pinch of cream of tartar
250 g (8 oz) caster sugar
1 teaspoon natural vanilla extract
fresh raspberries or grated high-cocoa-solid dark chocolate,
    to decorate (optional)

Filling
**Orange Cream (page 150) or other filling of your choice
(see opposite)**

Makes one 25 cm (10 inch) pie; serves 12

1 Preheat the oven to 130°C, 250°F, Gas Mark 1/2. Using a bowl or cake tin as a template, trace a 25 cm (10 inch) circle on to a piece of baking parchment, turn the paper over and use it to line a baking sheet.

2 Beat the egg whites in a large bowl with a hand-held electric mixer until foamy, then add the cream of tartar, and beat until the whites hold soft peaks. Continue beating as you add the sugar, 2 tablespoons at a time, until all of the sugar is incorporated and dissolved, and the meringue is glossy and holds firm peaks. Fold in the vanilla.

3 Dollop the meringue on to the circle drawn on the paper and, with the back of a large spoon, hollow out the centre and build up the edges. Bake in the oven for 1 hour, then lower the heat to 110°C, 225°F, Gas Mark 1/4 and bake for a further hour, until the meringue is beige, dry and crisp. Lift the meringue from the paper, and tap lightly with your finger – it should sound hollow. If it doesn't sound hollow, if the paper sticks, or if the meringue does not seem crisp, return it to the oven for another 20–30 minutes. When it is done, leave it in the turned-off oven for at least 1 hour.

4 Peel off the lining paper, and store the meringue shell in an airtight container until needed. When ready to serve, swirl in your chosen filling. Decorate with raspberries or grated chocolate, if you wish.

Eton Mess

CALORIE COUNT 139 KCAL FAT CONTENT <1G PER SERVING

If you have left-over meringues, crumble them and use them in this low-fat variation on a summer classic. The strawberries must be ripe and fabulous. If you have no left-over meringue, but still long for this famously shambolic version of meringues, strawberries and cream, buy a ready-made meringue but make sure it's a good one, made from real egg whites, not powder.

250 g (8 oz) very low-fat fromage frais

pulp from 1 vanilla pod (page 14), or $^1/_2$ teaspoon natural vanilla extract

$^1/_2$–1 tablespoon mild runny honey

500 g (1 lb) very ripe, flavourful strawberries, hulled

1 excellent-quality ready-made meringue shell, or left-over home-made meringue

light brown sugar, to sprinkle

Makes 750 ml (1$^1/_4$ pints); serves 4

1 Whisk together the fromage frais, vanilla pulp or extract and honey.
2 With a potato masher, mash half the strawberries in a bowl until they are a lumpy, juicy purée. Quarter the remaining strawberries.
3 Whisk the purée into the fromage frais. Crumble the meringue. Fold it, along with the strawberry quarters, into the fromage frais mixture. Serve in clear glass goblets or bowls. Top each serving with a sprinkling of brown sugar and allow to stand for a minute or so for the sugar to 'melt'.

Variation

Eton Mess with Peaches

1 Substitute ripe, juicy, flavourful peaches for the strawberries. Halve and stone the peaches (no need to peel), and dice them. Save a few of the peach cubes and put the rest into a bowl. Mash with a potato masher until they are slightly pulped and their juices are flowing.
2 Stir together the mashed peaches, their juices, vanilla and the fromage frais. Fold in the peach cubes and the crumbled meringue. Serve in glass goblets.

CHAPTER 5

FRUIT DESSERTS

When planning a healthy, low-fat dessert, fruit is the obvious choice, and, after all, we are constantly being urged, with great fanfare, to eat at least five servings of fruit and/or vegetables a day. Fruit does end things on a refreshing, vibrant and colourful note; perfect after a rich, spicy and complex meal. There are plenty of easy and fast fruit dessert ideas to throw together in no time at all, all of which will finish off a meal with great panache, even on busy days. Do take the time to choose beautifully ripe and fragrant fruit, otherwise the whole exercise is pointless.

Quick Fruit Desserts

- A sweet, ripe, aromatic melon (I'm partial to the orange-fleshed varieties) is glorious all on its own, or with just a squirt from half a fresh lime to bring things into focus. Alternatively, try melon halves with their cavities filled to overflowing with perfect raspberries or blueberries. Scoops of food-processor fruit sorbets (see page 89) are also perfect for the cavities of chilled melons.
- A mango just needs to be sliced into two pieces on either side of the stone, cubed to look like a hedgehog and turned inside out, then put on a pretty plate with a wedge of lime and a scattering of raspberries. Simple,

elegant, succulent and colourful, who could ask for anything more? Alternatively, try putting the flesh of a very ripe mango in a food processor with a carton of ricotta and a dash of natural vanilla extract (or the pulp of a vanilla pod), and process until perfectly smooth. Taste, and process in some icing sugar or honey, if necessary (it won't need much), and serve in goblets with a scattering of raspberries.

- I've had some dreadfully bad fruit salads in my life, which is a great shame because fruit salad can be the most sparkling and refreshing fruit dessert of all. I make it very simply, and rarely add any form of sweetener; if the fruit is seasonal, fresh and perfectly ripe, added sweetness is not really necessary. In the summer I like a selection of berries (blueberries, strawberries, raspberries), cubed peaches or nectarines, and halved, stoned cherries. Put them in a bowl, squeeze in the juice of $1/2$ orange and add a good dash of natural vanilla extract and a slosh of liqueur (orange-flavoured liqueur, such as Cointreau, is perfect). Serve as it is, or with a cloud of one of the creams (see pages 150–54).

- Single fruit salads can be dramatic and delicious: peaches in orange juice, vanilla and Crème de Pêche; oranges in orange juice and orange liqueur; halved, stoned cherries in orange and lemon juice, slivered zest, orange liqueur and vanilla. Halved strawberries are good in a syrup (I do use sugar here) of lime or lemon juice and a little sugar. When mixed together, the juice and sugar form a syrup that coats the berries nicely. In the winter, compotes of spiced dried fruit, in goblets with a blob of yogurt or ricotta cream (see pages 150–54), or ladled on to toast, are warming and comforting.

Apple and Pear Cranberry Crumble

CALORIE COUNT 353 KCAL FAT CONTENT 3G PER SERVING

The compote that forms the base of this crumble is lovely without the crumble, too, in goblets (warm or chilled) with one of the 'creams' (see pages 150–54), or heaped on to a toasted bread tart base (see page 143), again topped with a dollop of one of the creams.

750 g (1¹/₂ lb) tart eating apples
750 g (1¹/₂ lb) pears
90 g (3 oz) ready-to-eat dried apricots
75 g (2¹/₂ oz) package dried cranberries
juice of 1 orange
juice of about 2 lemons
1 tablespoon natural vanilla extract
3 tablespoons maple syrup
2 tablespoons lemon shred marmalade
6 pairs amaretti biscuits
90 g (3 oz) Grape Nuts cereal
1 whole egg
2 egg whites

Serves 6

1 Preheat the oven to 190°C, 375°F, Gas Mark 5.
2 Peel, core and dice the apples and pears, dice the apricots and mix together with the cranberries, citrus juices, vanilla, maple syrup and marmalade. Spread out in a baking dish and bake in the oven, uncovered, for 30 minutes, or until tender and juicy, stirring occasionally.
3 Meanwhile, put the amaretti biscuits and Grape Nuts in a food processor and process to fine crumbs. Add the egg and egg whites and process until well mixed.
4 Remove the compote from the oven, taste, and stir in more lemon juice, as needed, to balance the flavours.
5 Pour and scrape the crumble mixture over the compote, leaving a 1 cm (¹/₄ inch) border all around. Raise the oven temperature to 200°C, 400°F, Gas Mark 6 and bake the crumble for 10–12 minutes, until the topping is set and the juices are bubbling. Serve warm or at room temperature.

Caramelised Pears with Cannoli Cream

CALORIE COUNT 218 KCAL FAT CONTENT 4G PER SERVING

Pears are gorgeous baked, braised or sautéed. These are very attractive served in goblets with a thick layer of ricotta cream on top.

1 lemon
1 orange
4 firm, ripe pears
300 ml (^{1}/$_2$ pint) red vermouth
1 cinnamon stick
1 vanilla pod
^{1}/$_2$–1 tablespoon caster sugar
1 tablespoon orange-flavoured liqueur (Cointreau of Grand Marnier)
Cannoli Ginger or Orange Cream (pages 150–54)
shredded orange zest, to decorate

Serves 2

1 Squeeze the juice of half the lemon and half the orange into a bowl. Peel the pears, and dip them in the citrus juices to prevent browning. Halve and core the pears, and dip them again.
2 Cut each pear half in half again, and put them in a non-reactive frying pan with the citrus juice from the bowl. Finely pare the zest from 1/4 orange and 1/4 lemon, and cut into very fine strands. Add to the pan with the vermouth, cinnamon stick, vanilla pod, sugar and liqueur. Bring to the boil, then reduce the heat and simmer, uncovered, for 10–25 minutes or until the pear quarters are tender but not mushy, stirring frequently. With a skimmer or slotted spoon, remove the pears to a bowl, leaving the liquid behind.
3 Boil down the liquid until thickened and syrupy, then pour and scrape into a small jug. Return the pears to the frying pan, along with the juice of the remaining half lemon and orange.
4 Stir and cook quickly (and gently so that the pears do not break up) until the pears are richly glazed. Spoon the pears into glass goblets and pour some of the vermouth syrup over each. With a rubber spatula, dollop the cream into the goblets, and then spread it so it completely covers the pears. Decorate with some shreds of orange zest, and serve at once.

Pears Braised in Spiced Cabernet Sauvignon

CALORIE COUNT 107 KCAL FAT CONTENT <0.5G PER SERVING

The amount of sugar needed in this dish, and the cooking time required, depends on the sweetness and ripeness of the pears, so be flexible

juice of 1 orange
a few drops of lemon juice
6 firm, ripe pears
600 ml (1 pint) Cabernet Sauvignon
150 ml (5 fl oz) water
1 cinnamon stick, split
about 1 tablespoon sugar
1 piece stem ginger, chopped
1 tablespoon syrup from jar of stem ginger
1 star anise
1 vanilla pod, split

Serves 4

1 Squeeze the orange juice into a bowl and add a few drops of lemon juice. Peel the pears, but do not core them, and dip them into the citrus juices.
2 Put all the remaining ingredients, except the vanilla pod, in a saucepan that will comfortably hold the pears. Scrape the pulp from the vanilla pod and add it to the wine mixture. Throw in the scraped pod as well. Add the pears and citrus juices, and bring to the boil, then partially cover and simmer briskly, stirring occasionally, for 20–30 minutes or until the pears are tender but not mushy and are bathed in a syrupy wine reduction. If the liquid threatens to boil away before the pears are ready, add a little more water, as needed. Alternatively, if the pears are tender, and there is plenty of liquid left, scoop them out, put them in a bowl, and boil down the wine until thickened and syrupy. Taste carefully and add more sugar, or a few more drops of lemon juice, as needed.
3 When the pears are tender, put them in a bowl and strain the pan liquid over them. If you want a little more juice, return the strained solids (vanilla pod, cinnamon stick, ginger, star anise) to the saucepan, add more wine and water, a touch of sugar and ginger syrup and a few drops of lemon and orange juice, and boil until thickened and syrupy. Strain over the pears. Cover and refrigerate until needed.

New Wave Banoffee

CALORIE COUNT 282 KCAL FAT CONTENT 5G PER SERVING

My New Wave Banoffee was originally printed in my
Complete Low-Fat Cookbook, and (along with the food
processor ice creams and the tiramisù) has proved to be the
kind of recipe that turns people on, dessert-wise.

300 ml (^{1}/$_2$ pint) fresh orange juice

juice of ^{1}/$_2$ lemon

1^1/$_2$ tablespoons orange-flavoured liqueur (Cointreau or
Grand Marnier)

1–2 tablespoons dark brown muscovado sugar

5 ripe, firm bananas, peeled and sliced

2 x 250 g (8 oz) carton quark

250 g (8 oz) carton ricotta

2 tablespoons orange marmalade

2 tablespoons Grape Nuts cereal

2 amaretti biscuits

Serves 6

1 Combine the citrus juices, orange liqueur and 1 tablespoon sugar in a heavy-
bottomed saucepan. Bring to the boil, and boil, stirring, until syrupy and
reduced to a little less than half. Add the sliced bananas to the mixture, and
stir to coat thoroughly. Leave to cool slightly.
2 Put the quark, ricotta, marmalade and a little more sugar (if you feel it is
needed) in a food processor, and process until thoroughly combined.
3 Spoon the banana and orange mixture into individual glass goblets and top
with the creamy mixture.
4 Put the Grape Nuts and amaretti into a plastic bag. Pound with a kitchen
mallet or the bottom of a bottle to reduce to crumbs (or whirl them to crumbs
in a blender or small processor). Sprinkle evenly over the cream topping.

Variation

Banana Brulee Serves 4

Put the banana mixture into individual ramekins or baking dishes. Cover evenly
with a layer of very low-fat yogurt, then cover the yogurt with dark brown
sugar, also in an even layer. Flash under the grill for 1–2 minutes until the
sugar bubbles and melts.

Grilled Bananas

CALORIE COUNT 182 KCAL FAT CONTENT <0.5G PER SERVING

Dishes of bananas sautéed in butter and flamed in rum occur in several cuisines. This version grills them in orange juice with a touch of rum and brown sugar, for a similar delectably rich result. To shock and delight the senses, try serving each portion of the bananas piping hot with a scoop of cold creamy Banana and Ginger Ice Cream (see page 92) on top instead of the Lemon Brown Sugar Cream.

3 ripe bananas
juice of $1/2$ lime
juice of $1/2$ lemon
125 ml (4 fl oz) fresh orange juice
1 tablespoon dark rum
about 1 heaped tablespoon light brown sugar
1 tablespoon sultanas
Lemon Brown Sugar Cream (page 152), to serve

Serves 2-3

1 Preheat the grill to its highest setting.
2 Peel the bananas, cut them in half lengthways, then cut each half in half again, crossways.
3 Put the citrus juices and rum in a shallow baking dish that can hold the banana pieces in one layer. Turn the bananas in the juice. Arrange, cut sides down, in one layer, and sprinkle evenly with sugar.
4 Cook under the grill, 7.5 cm (3 inches) from the heat, for 3-5 minutes, or until the bananas are well browned on top.
5 Tilt the dish and drain the juices into a small saucepan or frying pan. Add the sultanas, and boil the juices to reduce by almost half.
6 Pour the juices back over the bananas, then divide between individual serving dishes. Top each hot portion with a dollop of Lemon Brown Sugar Cream.

Fruit Steeped in Red Wine

CALORIE COUNT 126 KCAL FAT CONTENT <0.5G PER SERVING

This was inspired by a recipe of Michel Guérard. It's remarkably refreshing and reviving on a hot summer's evening.

350 ml (12 fl oz) dry red wine (preferably a Bordeaux)
1 tablespoon natural vanilla extract
3 tablespoons caster sugar
175 ml (6 fl oz) water
750 g (1 1/2 lb) cherries or peeled and cubed peaches or raspberries
fresh mint leaves, to decorate

Serves 4

1 Put the wine, vanilla and sugar in a saucepan, bring to the boil, and boil until reduced by half. Add the water and bring back to the boil, then remove from the heat and leave to cool. Store in the refrigerator until needed.
2 To serve, divide the fruit among four large glass goblets. Pour the wine over the fruit, and allow to steep for a few minutes. Decorate with mint leaves before serving.

Simple Pleasures

For a remarkably refreshing, utterly simple summer thrill, slice dead ripe, lusciously fragrant peaches into goblets of chilled red wine. Obviously you should use a rough and ready red , not an exquisite vintage wine. Or try raspberries in a glass of very cold champagne, or – for the innocent – raspberries, halved stoned cherries or sliced peaches in icy Amé, American-style ginger ale or (oh, the sheer joy of it) vanilla flavoured seltzer (cream soda).

Fruit Ricotta Brulee

CALORIE COUNT 128 KCAL FAT CONTENT <0.5G PER SERVING

In this low-fat version of a great classic, the sugar melts under the grill, and then becomes brittle and glass-like (it shatters enticingly as you eat it). The yogurt and fromage frais mixture beneath remains smooth and cold, creating a lovely texture and temperature contrast. If you wish, bring this extravaganza down to size by using small individual ramekins or baking dishes.

250 g (8 oz) cherries, stoned and halved

125 g (4 oz) raspberries

250 g (8 oz) strawberries, hulled and halved

2 ripe peaches or nectarines, halved, stoned and sliced

250 g (8 oz) very low-fat natural yogurt

250 g (8 oz) very low-fat fromage frais

1 heaped tablespoon orange marmalade

1 teaspoon natural vanilla extract

about 8 tablespoons demerara sugar

Serves 8

1 Preheat the grill to high.
2 Arrange the fruit in a 20 cm (8 inch) square, 5 cm (2 inches) deep Pyrex or Pyroflam baking dish. Cover and refrigerate while you prepare the topping.
3 Whisk together all the remaining ingredients, except the demerara sugar, and spread the mixture over the fruit.
4 Sprinkle the sugar evenly over the top, and smooth with the back of a spoon. Grill, close to the heat, for 1/2–1 minute or until the sugar melts and bubbles. Allow to stand for a few moments before serving.

Fruit on Toast

Fruit on toast has become very trendy these days, although now everyone calls it *bruschetta*. (If it's Italian, it must be good.) It's a wonderfully warming, old-fashioned type of fruit pudding that can be as simple as a warm fruit compote ladled over a piece of toast, or a more elaborate, though equally warming, baked dish. Some simple fruit on toast ideas follow:

Toast some slices of good bakery white or wholemeal bread or a split *ciabatta*, or make a toast tart base (see page143). Ladle on:

- The Banoffee Banana Base (page 74)
- Apple and Pear Compote (page 71)
- Winter Dried Fruit Compote (page 88) with a dollop of one of the yoghurt or ricotta creams
- Caramelised Pears (page 72)
- Combine orange and grapefruit sections with a bit of orange juice, honey and grated zest. Top with some Raspberry Coulis (page 144) if you wish. (This is cold comfort, great for breakfast.)
- Bake 6-7 halved peaches in 4-6 oz marsala or medium sherry and a dash of vanilla and orange liqueur in a shallow baking dish (sprinkle them with some of the wine) for 15-20 minutes. Brush the toast with some of the juices, then boil down the remaning juices until syrupy. Put the peach halves on the toast, and drizzle the syrup over them.

Pineapple and Rum Toast

CALORIE COUNT 225 KCAL FAT CONTENT 1G PER SERVING

Fresh pineapple, in chunks in its own juices, is now easily available on the supermarket shelves. The amount of sugar needed in this recipe depends entirely on the sweetness of the pineapple and orange juice, and your own preference, so taste as you go.

600 ml (1 pint) orange juice
125 ml (4 fl oz) dark rum
$1/2$ teaspoon natural vanilla extract
juice of $1/2$ lime
grated zest of $1/2$ lime
light brown sugar, to taste (optional)
2 x 350 g (11$1/2$ oz) package fresh pineapple chunks
4 slices bakery white bread or rustic bread, toasted
lime wedges, to serve

Serves 4

1 Put the orange juice, rum, vanilla, lime juice and lime zest, and a little sugar to taste into a non-reactive frying pan. Drain any juices from the pineapple into the pan, then boil rapidly until reduced by about half. Taste the juices and stir in a little more sugar if they are too tart; a little more lime juice if too sweet.
2 Brush the toast liberally with some of the juices and place on serving plates. Add the pineapple to the juices and stir over a medium heat until warmed through. Scoop out the pineapple and ladle evenly over the toasts.
3 Boil down any remaining juices until thick and syrupy. Pour some of the syrupy juices over each toast and serve at once, with lime wedges.

Variation

Omit the toast. Serve the hot pineapple in goblets with scoops of icy pineapple sorbet (page 94).

Apple Clafoutis

CALORIE COUNT 266 KCAL FAT CONTENT <1G PER SERVING   (TRADITIONAL RECIPE CALORIE COUNT 300 KCAL FAT CONTENT 16G)

A clafoutis is a baked dish that looks like a fat, puffy, fruit-filled pancake. It's very easy to prepare, and when it emerges from the oven in all its puffed, bubbly glory, it provides the comfort of a freshly baked fruit pie, without the fat or pastry-wrestling involved in true pie-making.

oil and water spray (page 10)

100 g (3¹/₂ oz) plain flour

100 g (3¹/₂ oz) light brown soft sugar

3 tablespoons skimmed milk powder

pinch of freshly grated nutmeg

300 ml (¹/₂ pint) skimmed milk

6 tablespoons very low-fat natural yogurt

4 egg whites

2 teaspoons natural vanilla extract

1 tablespoon apricot conserve, melted

Fruit

625 g (1¹/₄ lb) Granny Smith apples, peeled, cored and coarsely diced

3 tablespoons sultanas or dried cranberries

pinch each of ground cinnamon and ground mace

about 2 tablespoons sugar (depending on the tartness of the apples)

2 tablespoons orange juice

1 tablespoon lemon juice

Serves 6

1 Preheat the oven to 190°C, 375°F, Gas Mark 5. Spray a 25 cm (10 inch) non-stick flan tin with oil and water. Put the apples and dried fruit in a bowl with the spices, sugar and citrus juices, and toss well together.

2 Sift the flour, sugar, milk powder and nutmeg into a bowl. In another bowl, whisk together the milk, yogurt, egg whites and vanilla. Pour the milk mixture into the flour mixture and stir until just mixed, with no lumps.

3 Pour the batter into the flan tin, and scatter the fruit and its juices over the top, leaving a 2.5 cm (1 inch) border all around. Bake in the oven for 30–40 minutes or until set, lightly browned and puffed. When it is almost done

(starting to puff and bubble), quickly and gently (without removing it from the oven) brush around the edges with the apricot conserve. When baked, cool on a rack; serve warm or at room temperature.

Variations

- Substitute blueberries for the apples, omit the sultanas or cranberries, cinnamon and mace, add a bit of grated lemon zest and cut the sugar down to 1/2–1 tablespoon (again, it depends on the tartness or sweetness of the berries). As this cooks, the berries burst, so the finished clafoutis looks as if there has been a purple explosion in your oven. Personally, I love it.
- Substitute halved stoned cherries for the apples, and omit the sultanas, cinnamon and mace. Add a few drops of natural almond extract.
- Substitute peaches or nectarines for the apples, omit the sultanas, cinnamon and mace, and add a dash (about 1/8 tablespoon) of natural almond extract.

'Comfort me with apples, for I am sick of love.'

Song of Solomon

Fruit Mille-Feuilles

CALORIE COUNT 335 KCAL FAT CONTENT 5G   (TRADITIONAL RECIPE CALORIE COUNT 765 KCAL FAT CONTENT 58G)

Filo – delicate and brittle leaves of pastry – comes in handy
for low-fat dessert cooks, but it is not nearly so versatile as
you might think. Personally, I think that it makes a lousy pie
crust, and it does tend to be fiddly and temperamental. I
like to use it for turnovers (see page 134), and these elegant
little mille-feuille stacks, otherwise I leave it alone.
Traditionally, filo is slathered with plenty of butter and oil –
a good lathering between each layer. I use it with lightly
beaten egg white, lightly beaten whole egg, or – as here –
oil spray. Always keep the filo leaves well covered with cling
film. (If you are a slow worker, cover with a barely damp tea
towel *over* the cling film.) Although fiddly, these are very
elegant, and the crispness of the pastry against the creamy
fruit filling is pleasurable. If frozen, thaw the filo – in its
package – overnight in the fridge.

> 300 g (10 oz) package filo pastry, thawed if frozen
> oil spray (see Note, opposite)
> filling of your choice (see opposite)

Serves 4

1 Preheat the oven to 200°C, 400°F, Gas Mark 6.
2 Unroll the filo and spread it out on your work surface. Cover with cling film.
  Using a 7.5 cm (3 inch) diameter glass as a template, and a sharp knife, cut
  eight circles from the stack of filo. (The stack will consist of approximately
  eight sheets of filo.)
3 Cover the circles with cling film. Spray a non-stick baking sheet with oil spray.
  Take one circle of filo leaves, separate the layers of the circle, and stack them,
  one on top of the other, on the sheet, spraying each one lightly with oil spray
  as you do so. Repeat with the remaining circles.
4 Bake in the oven for 5–8 minutes or until the circles are browned and slightly
  crisp, flipping the stacks over with a spatula about halfway through the baking
  time. When done, cool on a wire rack.
5 Put one stack of filo circles on a plate. Top with a generous cloud of filling, and

some fruit, and cover with another filo stack. Sift on a sprinkling of icing sugar, or icing sugar mixed with low-fat unsweetened cocoa powder. Serve at once.

Note

For this recipe, use a commercial oil spray (i.e. Pam or Frylite). A homemade oil and water spray (see page 10) will make the pastry leaves soggy.

Fillings for Mille-Feuilles

1 Chocolate Ricotta Mousse (page 116) topped with sliced bananas and crumbled amaretti.
2 Orange Cream (page 150) with fresh raspberries and grated high-cocoa-solid dark chocolate (grated to a powder on the small holes of a grater).
3 Cherry Cream (page 150) topped with Macerated Cherries and crumbled amarettl.
4 Amaretti Cherry Cheesecake Mousse and its topping (page 49).

Note

Different brands of filo come in different sizes, and different spellings – I've seen it spelled 'fillo', 'filo', and even 'phyllo'. Once you have baked your filo sheets, you may find yourself enchanted with the crunchy brown circles. I sometimes use them as crisps for dipping and snacking. Or use them to garnish sorbets and cheesecake mousse.

Apricot Palachinta

CALORIE COUNT 283 KCAL FAT CONTENT 1G PER SERVING   (TRADITIONAL RECIPE CALORIE COUNT 610 KCAL FAT CONTENT 40G)

Crêpes, lovely delicate thin pancakes, are perfect for
wrapping or folding around all sorts of fruit mixtures. I
particularly love the Hungarian practice of rolling them
around apricot purée. The original is topped with chopped
walnuts; I've substituted crushed amaretti. The unfilled
crêpes can be made in advance and refrigerated for a few
days, or frozen.

125 ml (4 oz) plain flour
2 tablespoons caster sugar
6 tablespoons skimmed milk powder
175 ml (6 fl oz) skimmed milk
4 egg whites
2 teaspoons natural vanilla extract
grated zest of 1 lemon and 1 orange
oil and water spray (page 10)
Dried Apricot Purée (page 148)
2 pairs amaretti biscuits, crushed

Makes 12–14 crêpes; serves 6

1 Sift the flour, sugar and milk powder into a bowl. Put the milk, egg whites,
   vanilla and citrus zests in a blender and blend until smooth. Whisk the liquid
   into the dry mixture to make a smooth batter. Leave to stand for 30 minutes.
2 Spray a non-stick 20 cm (8 inch) frying pan with oil and water, and heat over a
   high heat. When it sizzles, spray again, then reduce the heat to medium.
3 Using a ladle or scoop that holds about 60 ml (2 fl oz), transfer some batter to
   the hot pan. Immediately tilt and rotate the pan so that the batter spreads
   over the bottom in a thin layer. Cook over a high heat for a few seconds or
   until the batter bubbles a little and, with the help of a palette knife, you can
   grasp the edge of the crêpe and flip it over.
4 Cook the crêpe on the second side for a few seconds, until it is just set, slides
   around the pan easily and is speckled with gold underneath. Slide the crêpe on
   to a waiting sheet of greaseproof paper.
5 Repeat until all the batter is used. (If you are not using the crêpes straight
   away, stack them, interleaved with greaseproof paper, and refrigerate or freeze.
   Warm before using.)

6 To serve, spread some apricot purée on each crêpe and roll up. Put two or three crêpes on a plate, lying across each other, and sprinkle with the amaretti crumbs. Serve at once.

Variations

- Fill and roll with the Amaretti Cherry Cheesecake Mousse and topping (page 49).
- Spread each warm crêpe flat. Spoon some of the warm Banoffee Banana base (page 74) on a quarter of the crêpe. Fold over in half, and then in half again, so that the bananas are encased in a cone shape. Top with a scoop of Banana and Ginger Ice Cream (page 92).

Spiced Fig Compote

CALORIE COUNT 308KCAL FAT CONTENT 2G PER SERVING

Spicy, dark, ruby red vermouth and dried figs were meant for each other. Serve these as they are, or on toast (see page 78) with a dollop of Lemon Cream (see page 150).

500 g (1 lb) dried figs

250 ml (8 fl oz) red vermouth

1 tablespoon orange-flavoured liqueur (Grand Marnier or Cointreau)

juice and pared zest of $\frac{1}{2}$ orange, cut into fine shreds

pared zest of $\frac{1}{2}$ lemon, cut into fine shreds

1 cinnamon stick

1 vanilla pod

125 ml (4 fl oz) water

Makes 600 ml (1 pint); serves 4

1 Combine all the ingredients in a non-reactive saucepan.
2 Bring to the boil, then reduce the heat and simmer briskly, stirring occasionally, until the liquid has reduced to a thick syrupy glaze and the figs are plump and tender. Add a little more water if the liquid threatens to simmer away before the figs are ready.

Sweet Potato and Ginger Custard Torte

CALORIE COUNT 270 KCAL FAT CONTENT 2G PER SERVING

This is one of my most beautiful and subtly delicious recipes – I'm quite in love with it. It only works with orange-fleshed potatoes, so keep your eyes open for them. The compote can be served scattered on top, as directed, or as a garnish to each wedge. Sweet potatoes have both Caribbean and North American connections; the compote picks up on both. For a more elegant presentation, the torte may be made in a tin with a removable bottom. In this case, wrap the base of the tin in foil before baking, so that water from the water bath does not seep in.

625 g (1¼ lb) orange-fleshed sweet potatoes

1 piece stem ginger, chopped

2 tablespoons syrup from jar of stem ginger

½ tablespoon natural vanilla extract

grated zest of 1 lime and ½ orange

juice of ½ lime

1 tablespoon Dried Apricot Purée (page 148)

3 egg whites

215 g (7½ oz) can or carton light evaporated milk

1 Amaretti-Flavoured Crumb Crust (page 140) made in a 20 cm (8 inch) non-stick flan tin

Mango and Cranberry Compote (see opposite)

Serves 8

1 Preheat the oven to 190°C, 375°F, Gas Mark 5. Prick the potatoes in several places, then roast them in the oven for about 45 minutes or until they are very tender and spitting caramelised juices (put a tray on the oven floor to catch the sugary drips). Cool slightly, then strip off the skins and mash the flesh. Leave to cool.

2 Put the cooled mash in a food processor and purée until very smooth. While the processor is running, add the remaining ingredients (except the crumb crust and compote), one at a time, and continue processing until beautifully smooth.

3 Pour and scrape the sweet potato mixture on to the crumb crust in the flan tin and smooth the surface. Bake in the oven for about 35 minutes or until set (test with a cake tester). Leave to cool in the tin on a wire rack, then refrigerate.
4 At serving time, scatter the compote over the top of the torte.

Mango and Cranberry Compote

CALORIE COUNT 180 KCAL FAT CONTENT 1G PER SERVING

125 g (4 oz) dried mango pieces
75 g (2^1/$_2$ oz) dried cranberries
^{1}/$_2$ tablespoon natural vanilla extract
juice of 1–2 limes

Makes 600 ml (1 pint); serves 4

1 Roughly chop the mango pieces with scissors and put into a non-stick frying pan with the cranberries, vanilla and juice of 1 lime. Cover generously with water.
2 Bring to the boil, then reduce the heat and simmer, uncovered, for about 15 minutes or until the fruit is plumped and tender, and the liquid about gone. Towards the end, taste, and add more lime juice, as needed. When the fruit is tender, and bathed in a scant syrupy sauce, remove from the heat, leave to cool, then refrigerate until needed.

'The mango is unique and completely superior. It may be eaten out of the hand, gnawing at last on the great pit, or it may be cut daintily and served just so.'

Marjorie Kinnan Rawlings, *Cross Creek*

Winter Dried Fruit Compote

CALORIE COUNT 273 KCAL FAT CONTENT <1G PER SERVING

Don't use ready-to-eat (pre-soaked) fruit for any of the compotes, or they will turn to mush. I think a gently spiced dried fruit compote is an old-fashioned, splendidly comforting way to end a meal, especially topped with a blob of one of my 'creams'.

4 tablespoons sultanas

500 g (1 lb) mixed dried fruit (apricots, apples, figs, prunes, pears)

250 ml (8 fl oz) water

250 ml (8 fl oz) dry white wine

45 g (1¹/₂ oz) caster sugar

¹/₂ cinnamon stick

1 vanilla pod

juice and grated zest of 1 lemon

'cream' of choice (pages 150–54), to serve

Makes 600 ml (1 pint); serves 4

1 Combine the sultanas, fruit, water and wine in a baking dish and leave to soak for 1 hour.
2 Preheat the oven to 180°C, 350°F, Gas Mark 4.
3 At the end of the hour, stir the sugar into the fruit, and add the cinnamon stick, vanilla pod, lemon juice and lemon zest. Cover the dish and bake in the oven for 1 hour, stirring occasionally. Serve warm or cold with one of the 'creams'.

Note

Prunes on their own make a great compote. Of course, some people find prunes too ridiculous and dull for words, but if you love them as I do, try simmering ¹/₂ lb of them (not pre-soaked) in Lemon Verbena Tea (with a cinnamon stick, ¹/₂ a sliced lemon, the juice of ¹/₂ a lemon and ¹/₂ - 1 tablespoons of sugar), for 10-15 minutes, until plumped and fragrant. Serve with Honey Vanilla Cream (page 151).

CHAPTER 6

ICE CREAMS, SORBETS AND SUNDAES

Ice cream making at home is extraordinarily rewarding; you can indulge yourself in exquisitely pure ingredients, minimal butterfat, maximum taste, and whatever combination of weird and wonderful flavours strikes your fancy. There are several ways of making ice creams (and sorbets) at home. The first five recipes in this chapter are made using the 'instant food processor' method; the remainder use an ice cream maker or *sorbetière*, or the 'still freeze' method.

Instant Food Processor Ice Cream

I first developed this method back in the mid-seventies and it has now become something of a cliché, but it is so good, so easy, so much fun, that it would be madness to leave it out of this collection. You'll need a food processor (a small, inexpensive one works just fine) and a freezer. Simply freeze pieces of ripe fruit (berries, slices of peeled banana, chunks of pears, nectarines, peaches, mangoes, papayas – whatever looks good). Freeze the pieces flat on a baking sheet, then gather into plastic bags and store in the freezer until needed. The idea is to have separate, solidly frozen pieces, not a solid block; if the fruit pieces fuse together in a solid mass in the freezer; knock the bag sharply on the counter before using, to separate the pieces again.

To make the ice cream, put the frozen fruit pieces in a food processor, add 1 tablespoon sweetener (sugar, honey, marmalade or conserve, maple syrup or even a low-calorie sugar substitute like granulated Aspartame, for those who must limit their sugar consumption) add 1 tablespoon very low-fat fromage frais, yogurt or buttermilk, and process for about 1 minute until it is a lumpy, icy mass. Stop the machine, taste for sweetness, add more sweetener if necessary. Process again, scraping down the sides of the processor bowl and adding up to 1 tablespoon additional fromage frais, yogurt or buttermilk, as needed. Continue processing (about 3 minutes in total) until the mixture forms a smooth, creamy (no ice crystals) ice cream.

This gloriously creamy concoction is meant to be eaten almost at once; if stored in the freezer for much more than an hour, it becomes rock hard. In this case, leave it out for a few minutes to soften, but it will become icy rather than creamy. Perfection is *just made* processor ice cream. To make instant sorbet, follow the same method, but use fruit juice in place of fromage frais, yogurt or buttermilk.

Using these basics you can now go ahead and experiment with various combinations of fruit and sweeteners. There are several specific recipes in this chapter to get you started.

Electric Sorbetières and Ice Cream Makers

Is it worth buying one of these pricey machines? If you adore 'designer' ice creams (Ben and Jerry's, Häagen-Dazs, et al) and you want to enjoy the rich, multi-flavoured indulgences of such confections *without* the butterfat whammy, then yes, indeed it is. The machine delivers wonderful results: simply mix the ingredients, pour them in, and let the machine churn away. In no time at all the soft creamy frozen delight is ready. These machine-made ice creams *can* be stored in the freezer, but, because they contain minimal fat, most of them will freeze quite hard. There is an advantage to storing for a few hours or even a day or so: the ice cream ripens, that is the flavours develop, deepen and 'marry'. Soften in the refrigerator for 15 minutes or so, or, even better, zap them in the microwave for a few seconds. Ice creams and sorbets that contain liqueurs will *not* freeze rock hard – the alcohol keeps them softer.

If you are an ice cream addict and indulge in expensive high-fat ice creams often, it is very much worth buying a good machine. You will *lose* pounds, you will *save* pounds, and you will have the creative time of your life thinking up wonderful new ice cream flavours.

The Still Freeze Method

This is very fiddly, and the end result will be slightly grainy because some ice crystals will form, but it will enable you to try some of the ice cream machine recipes even if you have no machine. Make up the recipe and put it, in a metal bowl, in the freezer. Every hour or so, as the mixture begins to freeze, beat it with a hand-held electric mixer to break up the ice crystals. (Keep the beaters in the freezer.) Repeat several times until the mixture has frozen to ice cream consistency.

Banana and Ginger Ice Cream

CALORIE COUNT 138 KCAL FAT CONTENT <0.5G PER SERVING

To make the simplest banana ice cream in the world, simply put frozen sliced bananas in a food processor, and process, scraping down occasionally, until the bananas form a super-creamy ice cream. That's all! Strictly speaking, it's not an ice cream, but it sure tastes like one. This recipe is more elaborate – quite grown-up really! Serve it with Mango Sauce (see page 144) in pretty goblets.

6 ripe bananas (about 625 g/1¼ lb), peeled, sliced and frozen (see page 89)

1–2 tablespoons very low-fat fromage frais

1 tablespoon ginger conserve

1–2 tablespoons Chiquita Banana Drink or Banana–Orange Drink, (see Note, below) or orange juice

1 teaspoon natural vanilla extract

a splash of rum or Cointreau (optional)

a few drops of lime juice, to taste

Mango Sauce (page 144), to serve

Makes 900 ml (1½ pints); serves 5–6

1 Put the *still frozen* banana pieces in a food processor with 1 tablespoon fromage frais, 1 tablespoon conserve, 1 tablespoon banana drink or orange juice, the vanilla extract and the liqueur, if using. Turn the machine on.
2 Add another ½ tablespoon fromage frais and a few drops of lime juice, and process again. Stop the machine and scrape down the sides of the bowl, then start the machine again. When the mixture forms a super-creamy, smooth (no ice crystals), soft ice cream consistency, it is ready. Add a little more fromage frais and lime juice if necessary. Scrape the ice cream into a plastic container, cover, and store in the freezer for up to 1 hour. To serve, put a puddle of Mango Sauce in a goblet, and top with a scoop of the ice cream.

Note
Chiquita Banana Drink and Banana-Orange Drink are available in some large supermarkets; substitute orange juice if they are unavailable.

Peach or Nectarine Ice Cream

CALORIE COUNT 67 KCAL FAT CONTENT <0.5G PER SERVING

Peaches must be peeled (blanch in boiling water, then remove the skins) before they are cut into cubes and frozen (see page 89), but nectarines can be cubed and frozen, skins and all. In the summer, when peaches and nectarines are at their ripest, silkiest, perfumed best, buy masses, and freeze for future deep-winter blues. (If you don't eat ice cream in the middle of the winter, you're not a true ice cream fanatic.)

> 250 g (8 oz) frozen peach or nectarine cubes
> about 1 tablespoon peach (or apricot) conserve
> 1–2 dashes Crème de Pêche or Amaretto di Saronno (optional)
> 1 teaspoon natural vanilla extract
> 1–2 tablespoons very low-fat fromage frais
> 1 pair amaretti biscuits, crushed

Makes about 450 ml (³/₄ pint); serves 2–3

Make the ice cream according to the method described on page 90. Top each serving with amaretti crumbs.

Pear and Maple Ice Cream

CALORIE COUNT 57 KCAL FAT CONTENT <0.5G PER SERVING

Firm, not-quite-ripe pears are good for braising or roasting, but awful for ice cream. Buy very ripe, fragrant pears in season and cube and freeze in quantity for later use. (I usually don't bother to peel them.) Pear and Ginger is a wonderful combination too, so for a change, use stem ginger syrup (or ginger conserve) in place of the maple syrup.

> 250 g (8 oz) frozen pear cubes
> 1–2 tablespoons pure maple syrup
> a dash of Poire William (optional; only if you are lucky enough to have some around the house)
> 1–2 tablespoons very low-fat fromage frais

Makes about 450 ml (³/₄ pint); serves 2–3

Make the ice cream according to the method described on page 90.

Pineapple Rum Sorbet

CALORIE COUNT 39 KCAL FAT CONTENT <0.5G PER SERVING

Now that it is possible to buy ready-to-eat fresh pineapple chunks in the supermarket, this sorbet couldn't be easier. Pineapple is very sweet, so you don't need much preserves.

> 250 g (8 oz) frozen pineapple cubes
> a few drops of lime juice and orange juice
> ¹/₂–1 tablespoon pineapple preserves or pineapple and ginger conserve
> 1 tablespoon dark rum (optional)

Makes about 450 ml (³/₄ pint); serves 2–3

Make the sorbet according to the method described on page 90–91.

Cranberry and Orange Sorbet

CALORIE COUNT 63 KCAL FAT CONTENT <0.5G PER SERVING

Frozen cranberries are now available in many supermarkets, along with frozen raspberries, blueberries and summer fruits. Cranberries are very tart; you must sweeten this sorbet to taste. It is best, I think, if it remains a little tart – very refreshing and palate-cleansing after a rich, spicy meal. The colour is a most astonishing and exhilarating deep sunburst scarlet pink.

> 250 g (8 oz) carton frozen cranberries
> 1–2 tablespoons orange shred marmalade
> 1–2 tablespoons maple syrup
> 2–3 tablespoons cranberry juice drink

Makes 450 ml (³/₄ pint); serves 2–3

1 Put the cranberries in a food processor with 2 tablespoons marmalade, 1 tablespoon maple syrup and 1 tablespoon cranberry juice. Process to an ice-splintered mass, then stop and taste, and add more sweetener as needed.
2 Continue processing, adding just a bit more juice as needed, until the cranberries form a sorbet consistency. Store in the freezer for up to 1 hour.

Note

Cubes of fragrant mangoes and papaya, on their own, or together, make wonderful sorbets or ice cream. Whirl them in the food processor with just a dash of vanilla extract, if they are dead ripe, they will form the perfect creamy consistency without the help of fromage frais or buttermilk, or fruit juice.

Mocha-Maple Ice Cream

CALORIE COUNT 130 KCAL, FAT CONTENT 3G PER SERVING

The chestnut purée gives some body to this very low-fat ice cream, and the instant espresso coffee powder–cinnamon combo gives it an intoxicating high-class coffee-bar aroma.

125 g (4 oz) unsweetened chestnut purée
5 tablespoons pure maple syrup
60 g (2 oz) high-cocoa-solid dark chocolate, grated
1 teaspoon instant espresso coffee powder
1 teaspoon low-fat unsweetened cocoa powder
$1/8$ teaspoon ground cinnamon (or a touch more, to taste)
600 ml (1 pint) skimmed milk
3 tablespoons skimmed milk powder
1 tablespoon natural vanilla extract

Makes 1.25 litres (2 pints); serves 8

1 Combine all the ingredients in a blender, and blend until smooth but flecked with chocolate. Taste, and add a touch more cocoa, maple syrup or espresso powder, to taste. (Remember that freezing will blunt the flavour somewhat.)
2 Freeze in an ice cream maker according to the manufacturer's directions, or by the still freeze method (see page 91).

Right: Apple Clafoutis (page 80)

Chocolate Chestnut Rum Raisin Ice Cream

CALORIE COUNT 340 KCAL FAT CONTENT 6G PER SERVING

This makes a deep, dark, intense, sticky, chewy, completely outrageous and over-the-top chocolate ice cream. Because of the rum, it is scoopable straight out of the freezer. The only response to the first mouthful of this astounding ice cream is stunned silence. Its texture is extremely rich and so the ice cream is meant to be served in small scoops. Really, this is more of a gorgeous, frozen chocolate mousse than an ice cream.

90 g (3 oz) high-cocoa-solid dark chocolate, roughly chopped

410 g (13 1/2 oz) can sweetened condensed skimmed milk

4 tablespoons dark rum

3 tablespoons low-fat unsweetened cocoa powder, sifted

3 tablespoons sultanas

2 tablespoons natural vanilla extract

125 ml (4 fl oz) water

90 g (3 oz) unsweetened chestnut purée

1/5 pint skimmed milk

Makes 450 ml (3/4 pint); serves 6

1 Melt the chocolate in half the condensed milk and half the rum, in a microwave oven or in a heatproof bowl over a pan of simmering water. Whisk in the cocoa powder and leave to cool.

2 Briskly simmer the sultanas in the remaining rum, the vanilla and water for about 10 minutes or until they are plump, and the liquid has just about gone. Set aside to cool.

3 Put the chestnut purée in a blender with the chocolate, the skimmed milk and the remaining condensed milk. Blend until very smooth, stopping once or twice to scrape down the sides. Add the sultanas and pulse briefly to combine.

4 Freeze in an ice cream maker according to the manufacturer's directions.

Left: **Chocolate and Raspberry Cheesecake with fresh raspberries (page 44)**

Chocolate and Banana Sorbet

CALORIE COUNT 162 KCAL FAT CONTENT 1G PER SERVING

Although a sorbet rather than an ice cream, with remarkably low fat levels, this has all the dark, powerful depths of a killer, high-butterfat, designer ice cream. Although it's painfully hard to wait, the sorbet improves (the flavours intensify) if left overnight in the freezer. Three different sweeteners are used to build complex flavour, and a puréed banana *and* a sliced banana intensify the textural adventure.

90 g (3 oz) low-fat unsweetened cocoa powder

175 g (6 oz) light golden soft sugar

3 teaspoons instant espresso coffee powder

450 ml (³/₄ pint) warm water

1–2 tablespoons maple syrup

3 tablespoons orange marmalade

2 tablespoons dark rum

1 tablespoon natural vanilla extract

2 very ripe bananas

Makes 1.25 litres (2 pints); serves 8

1 Put the cocoa, sugar and espresso coffee powder in a saucepan. Whisk in the warm water, and bring to a simmer, stirring. Whisk in the maple syrup, marmalade, rum and vanilla, stirring until the marmalade has melted. Leave to cool, then chill.

2 Put the mixture in a blender, and peel and slice in one of the bananas. Blend to a lumpy purée, then transfer to a bowl. Slice the remaining banana very thinly, and stir in.

3 Freeze in an ice cream maker according to the manufacturer's directions, or by the still freeze method (see page 91).

Chocolate Sorbet

CALORIE COUNT 277 KCAL FAT CONTENT 2G PER SERVING

This sorbet, like the previous one, contains no dairy products at all, and no whole chocolate, yet it has breathtakingly dark chocolate depths that will strike you squarely in the centre of your chocolate-loving heart. I've printed this recipe before, in the (alas, now-out-of-print) *Slim Cuisine Italian Style* and, more recently, in *The Low-Fat Cookbook* (Dorling Kindersley, 1998), but it deserves to star in this collection as well.

> 250 g (8 oz) caster sugar
> 550 ml (18 fl oz) water
> 60 g (2 oz) low-fat unsweetened cocoa powder
> $1/2$ teaspoon natural vanilla extract

Makes 600 ml (1 pint); serves 4

1 Combine the sugar and water in a saucepan and heat gently until the sugar has dissolved. Raise the heat and boil for 1 minute, then remove from the heat and allow to cool slightly.
2 Stir in a little of the sugar syrup into the cocoa powder in a bowl, to make a smooth paste, then gradually stir in the remaining syrup. Add the vanilla. Strain the mixture through a fine sieve, then chill.
3 Freeze in an ice cream maker according to the manufacturer's directions, or by the still freeze method (see page 91).

Pear Ice Cream

CALORIE COUNT 57 KCAL FAT CONTENT NEG PER SERVING

A can of fruit, puréed in a blender with its juices, makes a splendid and convenient ice cream base. The fruit flavour is astonishingly fresh and pure. Pears sparked with lemon and made velvety by condensed milk are particularly successful.

400 g (14 oz) can pear halves in natural juice
1¹/₂ tablespoons lemon marmalade
1¹/₂ tablespoons sweetened condensed skimmed milk
¹/₂ tablespoon natural vanilla extract
grated zest of ¹/₂ small lemon

Makes 60 ml (1 pint); serves 4

1 Put all the ingredients in a blender, and blend until perfectly smooth.
2 Freeze in an ice cream maker according to the manufacturer's directions, or by the still freeze method (see page 91).

Mango Ice Cream

CALORIE COUNT 112 KCAL FAT CONTENT NEG PER SERVING

Canned mangoes, lime and vanilla form an enchanting tropical trio. Pair a scoop of this ice cream with a scoop of Lychee Sorbet (see page 101). Top with shreds of lime zest, and snippets of crystallised ginger.

400 g (14 oz) can mango slices in syrup
juice of 1 lime
1 teaspoon natural vanilla extract
2 heaped tablespoons very low-fat fromage frais

Makes 450 ml (³/₄ pint); serves 2–3

1 Put all the ingredients in a blender, and blend until smooth.
2 Freeze in an ice cream maker according to the manufacturer's directions, or by the still freeze method (see page 91).

Lychee, Lime and Ginger Sorbet

CALORIE COUNT 148 KCAL FAT CONTENT 0G PER SERVING

Very simple, with a heavenly fragrance, this sorbet – on its own or in concert with the pear and mango ice creams (see pages 100) is the perfect finish to a rich and substantial meal, or to a multi-course Chinese or Thai meal.

> 425 g (15 oz) can lychees in syrup
> 1/2 tablespoon syrup from a jar of stem ginger
> finely grated zest of 1/2 lime (use a zester)

Makes 300 ml (1/2 pint); serves 2

1 Put all the ingredients in a blender, and blend until perfectly smooth except for small flecks of lime zest.
2 Freeze in an ice cream maker according to the manufacturer's directions, or by the still freeze method (see page 91).

Hunza Apricot Ice Cream

CALORIE COUNT 115 KCAL FAT CONTENT <0.5G PER SERVING

Equal parts of very low-fat fromage frais and Hunza Apricot Purée (see page 146), flavoured with a smidgen of real vanilla, make an exceptionally aromatic, honeyed ice cream. My young (10-year-old) neighbour, Thomas, pronounced this the best ice cream he had ever tasted, with a very strong flavour of apricots. Clever boy.

> 300 ml (1/2 pint) very low-fat fromage frais
> 300 ml (1/2 pint) Hunza Apricot Purée (page 146)
> 1 teaspoon natural vanilla extract

Makes 750 ml (1 1/4 pints); serves 4–6

1 Whisk the ingredients together.
2 Freeze in an ice cream maker according to the manufacturer's directions, or by the still freeze method (see page 91).

Amaretti Ice Cream

CALORIE COUNT 190 KCAL FAT CONTENT <1G PER SERVING

Basic vanilla with the addition of crunchy, almond-scented amaretti crumbs and dried cherries – delightful!

$^1/_2$ quantity cherry and sultana compote (see step 1, page 49)

350 ml (12 fl oz) skimmed milk

125 ml (4 fl oz) sweetened condensed skimmed milk

1 teaspoon natural vanilla extract

2 amaretti biscuits, crushed

a few drops of lemon juice (optional)

Makes 600 ml (1 pint); serves 4

1 Put all the ingredients, except optional lemon juice, in a jug and whisk well.
2 Freeze in an ice cream maker according to the manufacturer's directions, or by the still freeze method (see page 91).
3 When the ice cream is almost done, taste it. If a bit too sweet for your taste, squeeze in a few drops of fresh lemon juice and finish freezing.

Coffee Ice Cream

CALORIE COUNT 118 KCAL FAT CONTENT NEG PER SERVING

Coffee is one of the great classic ice cream flavours. Eliminate the caffeine, if you wish, by using decaffeinated coffee.

300 ml ($^1/_2$ pint) strong, brewed coffee, chilled

175 ml (6 fl oz) sweetened condensed skimmed milk

zest of $^1/_4$ lemon

$^1/_4$ teaspoon ground cinnamon

$^1/_2$ teaspoon natural vanilla extract

Makes 600 ml (1 pint); serves 4

1 Combine all the ingredients in a jug. (Zest the lemon over the jug, so that the lemon oil goes into the liquid.)
2 Freeze in an ice cream maker according to the manufacturer's directions, or by the still freeze method (see page 91).

Grape Nut Cinnamon Crunch Ice Cream

CALORIE COUNT 102 KCAL FAT CONTENT <0.5G PER SERVING

Vanilla again, but with a little cinnamon and a Grape Nuts crunch. Grape Nut Ice Cream is an endearing folk-art-type traditional recipe from New England. When I lived in New England I grew to love it right up there with log cabins, crazy quilts, Shaker furniture and Indian pudding.

350 ml (12 fl oz) skimmed milk
125 ml (4 fl oz) sweetened condensed skimmed milk
1 teaspoon natural vanilla extract
2 tablespoons Grape Nuts cereal
$^1/_2$ teaspoon ground cinnamon
1 tablespoon demerara sugar
a few drops of lemon juice (optional)

Makes 750 ml (1$^1/_4$ pints); serves 4–6

1 Combine all the ingredients, except the sugar and the optional lemon juice, in a jug and whisk well.
2 Freeze in an ice cream maker according to the manufacturer's directions, or by the still freeze method (see page 91). When the ice cream is almost ready, sprinkle in the brown sugar (to add exquisite crunch). Taste and add a few drops of fresh lemon juice, if the ice cream seems a bit too sweet, then finish freezing.

Ice Cream Sundaes

The ice cream sundae first appeared early in the century and, I must say, it is one of the great dessert concepts of the twentieth century. It was invented in America, which is why – at its unfettered best – it is completely over the top. First some syrup goes into a chilled metal goblet, then several scoops of ice cream, topped with a deluge of hot fudge sauce or marshmallow fluff (cooked meringue). Crushed sweetened pineapple, raspberries or strawberries are drizzled in next, followed by the obligatory clouds of whipped cream. The whole thing is crowned with a scattering of nuts in more syrup, chocolate sprinkles (referred to as 'jimmies' in New England – I never found out why) and a single maraschino cherry (or several if the counter man is in a good mood).

There is no reason not to bring an up-to-date version of this study in excess into the new century. To be good, a sundae has to be made with pure and vibrant ingredients, but why shouldn't they be low-fat and healthy as well?

Elegant Sundae Ideas

- Hot Pineapple (page 79) topped with Pineapple Rum Sorbet (page 94).

- Peach Ice Cream (page 93) topped with crushed ripe peaches and a drizzle of Amaretto di Saronno and amaretti crumbs.

- Grilled Bananas (page 75) topped with Banana and Ginger Ice Cream (page 92) and snippets of crystallised ginger.

- Caramelised Pears (page 72) topped with Pear and Maple Ice Cream (page 94).

- Chocolate Chestnut Rum Raisin Ice Cream (page 97) topped with raisins and sultanas simmered until plump in a little dark rum and orange juice, blanketed in Hot Chocolate Fudge Sauce (page 118) (be still my palpitating heart!).

- A split banana topped with Chocolate and Banana Sorbet (page 98) and food processor raspberry sorbet (page 89). Pour on some Raspberry Coulis (page 144) and top with crushed amaretti biscuits.

- Mango Ice Cream (page 100) with Mango Sauce (page 144) and Exotic Fruit Salad (page 58) and shredded lime zest.

- Hunza Apricot Ice Cream (page 101) in Hunza Apricot Purée (page 146) with diced dried apricots simmered until plump in a little orange juice and Cointreau. Top with shredded orange zest.

All of these new wave sundaes have a certain restrained purity about them, but tip them into excess if you wish, by topping each with one of the 'creams' (pages 150–54) flavoured to complement, e.g. peach preserves for the peach sundae, maple syrup for the pear sundae, and so on.

CHAPTER 7

CHOCOLATE DESSERTS

Every once in a while, I meet someone who just doesn't like chocolate, and I muse: 'Hmmm – I'm sure this person has many good qualities, but *really* . . .' A life without chocolate just doesn't seem complete somehow. There is something about its dark, smooth, naughty richness that administers to a need deep within the recesses of our souls . . . Forgive me! Every time I write about chocolate, I go all funny and strangely metaphysical. I have no idea what I'm talking about; I just know that I love it, I want it, I need it. I'm not a chocoholic; I can go for days, even weeks, without a taste of the magical stuff, but I love knowing that it is there waiting for me, when I feel the urge.

To wallow in low-fat chocolate confections, you must get into the kitchen and do it yourself. Cocoa powder is chocolate with a significant amount of the cocoa butter removed. Excellent cocoa powder, even lower in fat than that found in the supermarket, is available by mail order (see page 156). It has a deep, dark chocolate richness that is most satisfying. Whole, dark chocolate, high in cocoa solids (therefore lower in fat) is fabulous as well – add it to many cocoa-based desserts in tiny quantities for extra flavour and richness. A mere 15 g (^{1}/$_2$ oz) can deliver powerful chocolate depths. The whole chocolate you choose should have at least 60 per cent cocoa solids, and should contain *no* vegetable fat.

Melting chocolate

Chocolate must be melted carefully. There are two potential pitfalls: scorching and seizing.

Scorching

To avoid scorched chocolate, melt it in a *bain-marie*, a heatproof glass or metal bowl set over a pan of simmering water. The surface of the water must be at least 1 cm (^{1}/$_2$ inch) below the base of the bowl, and the water should not actually boil.

A microwave oven works well, too: put the chocolate into a bowl and zap it for 60 seconds. If not melted, re-zap for a few seconds at a time, checking after each zap.

Seizing

A small amount (less than 1 tablespoon per 30 g/1 oz) of moisture added to chocolate as it melts will cause it to 'seize' and become grainy and lumpy – horrible! This is why the water under the *bain-marie* must remain below the bottom of the bowl, and must not boil. Droplets of steam falling into the chocolate will cause havoc. Make sure that your utensils are perfectly dry; a wet wooden spoon used to stir the melting chocolate will cause similar problems. Paradoxically, you *can* melt chocolate in liquid, as long as it is more than 1 tablespoon per 30 g (1 oz).

Dipping

Melted high-cocoa-solid dark chocolate just begs to be dabbled in. Line a baking sheet (or several) with baking parchment and start dipping. Try the following. Dip each halfway in and place on the baking tray to dry and harden. Serve as petits four in small pleated paper cases, or use to decorate cakes or sundaes.

- cubes of crystallised ginger

- amaretti biscuits

- bite-sized shredded wheat

- Almond Biscuits (page 142)

- fresh strawberries on the stem (they must be perfectly dry before dipping)

- cherries on the stem (perfectly dry)

- ready-to-eat dried apricot halves

- ready-to-eat dried figs

- ready-to-eat prunes, but instead of dipping them, mix some of the melted chocolate with a little low-fat soft cheese, slit the ready-to-eat stoned prunes and stuff the prunes with the chocolate cheese

- ready-to-eat dried pear halves

- dried sweet cherries

Old-Fashioned Dark Chocolate Pudding or Spread

CALORIE COUNT 168 KCAL FAT CONTENT 2G PER ¹/₄ PINT   (TRADITIONAL RECIPE CALORIE COUNT 241 KCAL FAT CONTENT 20G)

This works as a pudding to serve in bowls (with a dollop of one of the 'creams' (see pages 150–54) on top if you wish), or a spread to fill roulades or layer cakes, or an icing to slather on filled cakes and roulades. It is very versatile, very dark and rich tasting, and exceptionally more-ish. It doesn't have a milk-chocolate taste at all, but a dark, deep and intense one for true chocolate connoisseurs. If you have a microwave oven, use it – it guarantees a scorch-free pudding (see below).

> 8 tablespoons low-fat unsweetened cocoa powder
> 15 g (¹/₂ oz) high-cocoa-solid dark chocolate, grated
> 8 tablespoons caster sugar
> 4 tablespoons cornflour
> tiny pinch of salt
> 900 ml (1¹/₂ pints) skimmed milk
>
> Makes 1 litre (1³/₄ pints); serves 7

1 Put all the ingredients in a bowl and whisk together. Transfer to a blender, and blend until *very* smooth.
2 Rinse a heavy-bottomed, non-stick saucepan with cold water. Pour out the water, but do not dry the saucepan (this helps reduce scorching). Pour the chocolate milk mixture into the pan and heat over a medium heat, stirring, until it begins to bubble strenuously. As you stir, do not scrape the bottom of the pan; if any scorching does occur, you do not want to stir the scorched bits into the pudding. Reduce the heat, and continue stirring and cooking for 1 minute, until richly thickened. Remove from the heat.
3 Immediately pour the mixture into a bowl, cover with non-PVC (microwave) cling film, directly on the surface of the pudding, cool and refrigerate until needed.

Microwave Chocolate Pudding or Spread

CALORIE COUNT 152 KCAL FAT CONTENT 2G PER ¼ PINT

9 tablespoons low-fat unsweetened cocoa powder

3 tablespoons cornflour

5 tablespoons skimmed milk powder

8 tablespoons caster sugar

15 g (½ oz) high-cocoa-solid dark chocolate, grated

½ teaspoon natural vanilla extract

about 550 ml (18 fl oz) skimmed milk (1 long-life carton)

Makes 1.25 litres (2 pints)

1 Spoon the cocoa, cornflour, milk powder and sugar into a 2 litre (3½ pint), 18 cm (7 inch) top diameter, opaque white plastic or Pyrex glass measuring jug. Sprinkle in the grated chocolate.

2 Using a wire whisk, whisk the vanilla and milk into the dry ingredients. Whisk well to remove any lumps and to reduce the risk of 'volcanic eruptions' in the microwave. Cover the jug tightly with a plate.

3 Microwave on full power for 3 minutes. Carefully uncover (averting your face and taking care – the steam is hot) and whisk thoroughly. Re-cover and microwave on full power for another 2 minutes. Carefully uncover, whisk, re-cover and microwave for a final 1½–2 minutes, until boiled, thickened and smooth.

4 Whisk and let stand for 5 minutes, whisking occasionally. Cover with a sheet of non-PVC (microwave) cling film, directly on the surface of the pudding, leave to cool, then store in the refrigerater until required.

Banana and Chocolate Cream Pie

CALORIE COUNT 281 KCAL FAT CONTENT 2G PER SERVING

The preceding chocolate puddings are endlessly useful. Here, it fills a meringue shell, under a layer of banana slices. I find myself ever-so-slightly breathless as I write about this – it's almost too much to contemplate! Fill the shell at serving time; the meringue will disintegrate if the pie is left to wait too long.

2–3 tablespoons orange marmalade

3 firm, ripe bananas (not under-ripe, but not yet blotched and squishy)

1 meringue pie shell, thoroughly cooled (page 66)

about $1/2$ quantity Old-Fashioned Dark Chocolate Pudding (page 109)

a few tablespoons Orange Cream (page 150)

1 tablespoon grated high-cocoa-solid dark chocolate

Serves 8

1 Put the marmalade in a frying pan and heat gently to melt. Peel and slice the bananas and gently stir them into the marmalade until well coated. Set aside.
2 Put the meringue on a large round platter. Gently swirl in the chocolate pudding.
3 Put a circle of banana slices around the perimeter of the pie and artistically arrange the remainder in a heap in the centre. Pipe on rosettes of the cream, or spoon on picturesque dollops. Sprinkle chocolate on the rosettes or dollops and on the bananas. Serve at once.

Variation

Chocolate Bananna Bruschetta

This is a quick-and-dirty version of Banana and Chocolate Cream Pie – very childish and very satisfying. Lavishly spread dark chocolate pudding on thick slices of lightly toasted *ciabatta* or crusty, rustic French bread. Top with bananas in melted marmalade, as in step 1, above. The bananas should completely cover the surface. Brush with a little more melted marmalade. Flash *briefly* (a few seconds) under the grill, and eat at once.

Killer Chocolate Chestnut Layer Cake

CALORIE COUNT 275 KCAL FAT CONTENT 5G PER SERVING   (TRADITIONAL RECIPE CALORIE COUNT 1181 KCAL FAT CONTENT 86G)

Chocolate extract is a no-fat essence of chocolate, and is very powerful and intense. It is available by mail order (see page 156) if you can't get it locally. If you have none and just can't wait, the cake will still be amazingly delicious, fudgy and dark – not quite as earth-shakingly, deeply fudgy perhaps, but terrific none the less.

90 g (3 oz) plain flour

6 tablespoons low-fat unsweetened cocoa powder

270 g (9 oz) caster sugar

10 egg whites (at room temperature)

pinch of cream of tartar

1 teaspoon natural vanilla extract

1 teaspoon chocolate extract (see above)

45 g (1¹/₂ oz) high-cocoa-solid dark chocolate, grated

Chocolate Chestnut Spread (page 116)

Serves 8-10

1 Preheat the oven to 180°C, 350°F, Gas Mark 4. Line two 20 cm (8 inch) sandwich cake tins with baking parchment.
2 Sift the flour, cocoa powder and 100 g (3¹/₂ oz) of the sugar into a bowl.
3 Put the egg whites in a large bowl and beat with a hand-held electric mixer until foamy. Add the cream of tartar and beat until the whites hold soft peaks. Continue beating, adding the remaining sugar, 2 tablespoons at a time, until the sugar is dissolved and the whites are stiff and glossy. Fold in the vanilla, chocolate extract and 30 g (1 oz) of the grated chocolate.
4 A little at a time, sprinkle the sifted flour and sugar mixture over the egg white mixture and fold in gently but thoroughly.
5 Gently spoon the mixture into the prepared tins and smooth the tops. Bake in the oven for about 15–20 minutes or until the tops spring back when gently pressed with your finger, and a cake tester inserted in the centre of each cake comes out clean.
6 Leave to cool in the tins on a wire rack, then gently remove from the tins and peel off the lining paper. Be careful – they are very fragile. Split each one in

half to form 4 layers.

7 Put a layer on a plate and slather with chocolate chestnut spread and top with another layer. Continue until all the layers are stacked. Spread a layer of chocolate chestnut spread on top, and sprinkle with the remaining grated chocolate, cover and refrigerate until needed.

Variation

Squidgy Layer Cake

Bake for 10–15 minutes only, until the cake is still a bit sticky and a cake tester comes out not quite clean. Don't split each layer into two, but fill the layers with chocolate chestnut spread and sprinkle the top with grated chocolate.

Alternative fillings

Fill with the Chocolate Spread (page 109). Glaze the top with Apricot Glaze (page 154).

Fill with Chocolate Ricotta Mousse or Amaretti Cheesecake Mousse. Top with grated chocolate or cherry jam glaze.

Double Chocolate Soufflé

CALORIE COUNT 152 KCAL FAT CONTENT 2G PER SERVING   (TRADITIONAL RECIPE CALORIE COUNT 274 KCAL FAT CONTENT 16G)

I like my chocolate soufflé to remain moist inside; at the end of cooking a cake tester carefully inserted into one of the cracks will not test quite clean (test when the soufflé is still in the oven, and open and close the oven door *very* gently). This is one of the great chocolate experiences of all time. Serve as it is, or with Raspberry Coulis (see page 144), or even (oh, the joy of excess) with Hot Chocolate Fudge or Chocolate Sauce (see pages 117–18).

9 tablespoons caster sugar

9 tablespoons low-fat unsweetened cocoa powder

9 egg whites (at room temperature)

pinch of cream of tartar

15 g (^{1}/$_2$ oz) high-cocoa-solid dark chocolate, grated

1^1/$_2$ teaspoons natural vanilla extract

1^1/$_2$ teaspoons dark rum

Serves 6

1 Preheat the oven to 180°C, 350°F, Gas Mark 4.
2 Set aside about 2 tablespoons of the sugar, and sift the remainder with the cocoa powder into a bowl. Set aside.
3 Put the egg whites in a large bowl with the cream of tartar and beat with a hand-held electric mixer until foamy. With the machine on its highest speed, continue beating, adding the 2 tablespoons plain sugar, a little at a time, until the whites hold stiff peaks.
4 With a rubber spatula, fold the sifted sugar and cocoa mixture into the beaten whites. Fold in the grated chocolate, vanilla and rum.
5 Pile the mixture into a 3.5 litre (6 pint) soufflé dish. Bake in the centre of the oven (remove the top shelf first) for approximately 30 minutes or until dramatically risen and cracked, but still a bit moist inside. Serve at once.

Collapsed Double Chocolate Torte with Cherries or Raspberries

CALORIE COUNT 183 KCAL FAT CONTENT 3G PER SERVING

Bake your chocolate soufflé in a cake tin, let it collapse, and you will have a ravishingly squidgy, deeply chocolatey cake.

9 tablespoons caster sugar

9 tablespoons low-fat unsweetened cocoa powder

9 egg whites (at room temperature)

pinch of cream of tartar

1 1/2 teaspoons natural vanilla extract

1 1/2 teaspoons dark rum

15 g (1/2 oz) high-cocoa-solid dark chocolate, grated

cherries or raspberries and 1 tablespoon grated dark chocolate, to serve

Serves 6

1 Preheat the oven to 180°C, 350°F, Gas Mark 4.
2 Set aside about 2 tablespoons of the sugar, and sift the remainder with the cocoa powder into a bowl.
3 Put the egg whites in a large bowl with the cream of tartar and beat with a hand-held electric mixer until foamy. With the machine on its highest speed, continue beating, adding the 2 tablespoons plain sugar, a little at a time, until the whites hold stiff peaks.
4 With a rubber spatula, fold the sifted sugar and cocoa mixture into the beaten whites. Fold in the vanilla, rum and grated chocolate.
5 Pile the mixture into a 20 cm (8 inch) square loose-bottomed cake tin. Bake in the centre of the oven for 20–30 minutes or until a skewer inserted near the centre emerges not quite clean. Remove from the oven and leave to cool on a wire rack.
6 When the torte is cooled and collapsed, remove the sides of the tin and put the torte on a large platter. Pile some cherries or raspberries in the centre of the cake and sprinkle with the 1 tablespoon grated chocolate. Surround the cake with the rest of the fruit, and serve.

Note

For the cherries and berries, gently toss fresh raspberries with a soupçon of Framboise or Cointreau, or stoned, halved cherries with Cointreau, and a touch of Amaretto de Saronno.

Chocolate Chestnut Filling or Spread

CALORIE COUNT 303 KCAL FAT CONTENT 11G PER ¼ PINT

A mocha-coloured, richly textured spread, to fill the chocolate layers (see page 23), small meringues (see page 64) or a chocolate roulade (see page 27). The chestnut purée and condensed milk give the filling spectacular body.

250 g (8 oz) unsweetened chestnut purée

120 g (4 oz) high-cocoa-solid dark chocolate, melted (page 107)

2 tablespoon low-fat unsweetened cocoa powder

6 tablespoons sweetened condensed skimmed milk

1½ tablespoons natural vanilla extract

2 x 200 g (7 oz) carton low-fat soft cheese

Makes 500 ml (¾ pint)

Put all the ingredients in a food processor and process until perfectly smooth. Transfer to a bowl, cover and chill until required.

Chocolate Ricotta Mousse

CALORIE COUNT 260 KCAL FAT CONTENT 11G PER ¼ PINT

Layer this in a trifle (see page 55) or drain overnight in a dampened butter-muslin-lined sieve and then swirl into a meringue crust (see page 66), or a chocolate crumb crust (see page 140). Top with raspberries and grated chocolate.

Hot Chocolate Fudge Sauce (page 118), cooled

2 x 250 g (8 oz) carton ricotta

Put the cooled sauce in a food processor with the ricotta, and process until smooth.

Chocolate Sauce

CALORIE COUNT 47 KCAL FAT CONTENT <1G PER TABLESPOON

This is the sort of silky, dark-yet-innocent chocolate sauce used to make Chocolate Milk: a puddle of sauce in a tall glass, a sluice of ice-cold milk, a long-handled silver spoon to stir with a satisfying clatter, *et voilà*: nectar. Go a bit further and make the *vin ordinaire* of the vanished candy stores of New York's Lower East Side, the Egg Cream: the same puddle of sauce, tall glass and long spoon, a splash of milk and a deluge of cold seltzer (carbonated water) squirted from a siphon held high above the glass (no eggs, no cream, go figure!). Squirt like mad and stir like mad until you create a gorgeous head of chocolate foam, and drink at once. Pure heaven! Of course, you can abandon these childish ideas and serve the sauce over meringues or ice cream.

250 g (8 oz) caster sugar
175 ml (6 fl oz) water
90 g (3 oz) low-fat unsweetened cocoa powder
1 tablespoon natural vanilla extract
30 g (1 oz) high-cocoa-solid dark chocolate, grated
about 2 tablespoons maple syrup

Makes 450 ml (³/₄ pint)

1 Put the sugar and water in a heavy-bottomed non-stick saucepan, and bring to the boil. Boil for 2 minutes, then remove from the heat and leave to cool slightly.

2 Add the cocoa to the sugar syrup, and whisk hard with a wire whisk until the sauce is perfectly smooth. Stir in the vanilla and beat in the grated chocolate. Return to the heat and cook over a medium heat, stirring, for 1–2 minutes. Remove from the heat once again.

3 Beat in the maple syrup, to taste. Serve hot or cold. (It will keep for weeks in the fridge.)

Hot Chocolate Fudge Sauce

CALORIE COUNT 42 KCAL FAT CONTENT <0.5G PER TABLESPOON

Less intense and less childish than the preceding sauce, this is meant to be layered in trifles and sundaes, or processed with ricotta to make a Chocolate Ricotta Mousse (see page 116).

45 g (1¹/₂ oz) low-fat unsweetened cocoa powder

100 g (3¹/₂ oz) caster sugar

8 tablespoons skimmed milk powder

125 ml (4 fl oz) cold water

1 teaspoon natural vanilla extract

15 g (¹/₂ oz) high-cocoa-solid dark chocolate, grated

Makes 300 ml (¹/₂ pint)

1 Sift together the cocoa, sugar and milk powder, and put in a blender with the water, vanilla and grated chocolate. Blend, stopping frequently to scrape down the sides, until very well combined and perfectly smooth.

2 Rinse a heavy-bottomed, non-stick saucepan with cold water. Pour out the water, but do not dry the saucepan (this helps reduce scorching). Strain the mixture into the pan and heat over a medium heat, stirring, until it begins to bubble strenuously. As you stir, do not scrape the bottom of the pan; if any scorching does occur, you do not want to stir the scorched bits into the pudding. Continue stirring for 1 minute, then remove from the heat.

3 If the hot sauce is not being used immediately, pour into a bowl and cover with non-PVC (microwave) cling film, directly on the surface of the sauce. Leave to cool, then refrigerate until needed. To reheat, transfer to a saucepan and heat very gently, stirring constantly.

Variation

Microwave Hot Chocolate Fudge Sauce

1 Follow Step 1 above, then scrape the mixture into a 2 litre (3¹/₂ pint) heatproof glass bowl or measuring jug. Cover with a plate.

2 Microwave on full power for 1 minute, then uncover carefully and whisk well. Re-cover and microwave for 30 seconds, then whisk again. Re-cover and microwave for another 30 seconds, then uncover and whisk once more.

3 If not being used immediately, cover, cool and refrigerate as in step 3, above. Reheat in 1-minute bursts in the microwave.

CHAPTER 8

OLD-FASHIONED PUDDINGS

Food is comfort, and few gastronomic comforts compare with the sweet carbohydrate fix of old-fashioned 'nursery' puddings. Bread and butter puddings and rice puddings are particularly evocative of childhood, and, for me, noodle pudding is even more so. All these desserts, in their traditional form, are about as creamy and buttery as desserts can possibly be; we long for the comfort but recoil from the fat Calories.

I love bringing these puddings up to date. Add a little booze here and there (we're adults now, after all), and cut the fat drastically, but leave all the voluptuous comfort, and the occasional culinary return to the nursery will do no harm at all.

Apricot Bread and Unbutter Pudding

CALORIE COUNT 185 KCAL   FAT CONTENT 2G PER SERVING

I never get tired of making bread puddings. Although my versions are very low in fat, they deliver superb sweet comfort. Bread puddings can be made with cubed or sliced bread, usually tender white, but occasionally I use slices from a close-textured substantial loaf (Pain au levain) for a totally different effect. The tender white bread soaks up the custard as it cooks so that the pudding emerges puffed up like a soufflé; the Pain au levain remains rather chewy, with a creamy layer of custard beneath. The pudding will still be puffed rather dramatically but the bread will not be quite so saturated with custard. Both are terrific – it just depends what you are in the mood for.

6 slices fresh or one-day-old good-quality white bread

250 g (8 oz) package ready-to-eat dried apricots, diced with scissors

2 whole eggs

3 egg whites

1 tablespoon natural vanilla extract

3 tablespoons no-added-sugar, high-fruit apricot spread

3 tablespoons skimmed milk powder

500 ml (16 fl oz) skimmed milk

1–2 tablespoons demerara sugar

Serves 6–8

1   Cut the bread into quarters and arrange, in two overlapping rows, in the bottom of a 20 x 30 cm (8 x 12 inch) baking dish. Tuck the apricot pieces under and in between the bread slices.

2   Put the eggs, egg whites, vanilla and fruit spread in a blender and blend well. Whisk the skimmed milk powder into the milk and pour into the blender. Blend until foamy, then pour the mixture over the bread. With a broad spatula, push the bread down into the liquid and leave it to soak while you preheat the oven to 180°C, 350°F, Gas Mark 4. Put the kettle on to boil.

3 Sprinkle the sugar evenly over the bread. Stand the baking dish in a larger baking dish or roasting tin, and pour enough boiling water into the larger dish or tin to come halfway up the sides of the smaller dish. Bake in the oven for 45–55 minutes or until puffed, golden and set (a knife inserted near the centre will come out clean).

Custard Rice Pudding

CALORIE COUNT 283 KCAL FAT CONTENT 4G PER SERVING   (TRADITIONAL RECIPE CALORIE COUNT 442 KCAL FAT CONTENT 26G)

Very childish: sweet, creamy, tender – unparalleled comfort.

175 g (6 oz) Jasmine rice or Thai fragrant rice
1 cinnamon stick, broken in 2 pieces
grated zest of 1 orange and 1 lemon
2 whole eggs
3 egg whites
405 g (13 oz) can sweetened condensed skimmed milk
300 ml ($^1/_2$ pint) light evaporated milk
1 tablespoon natural vanilla extract

Serves 8

1 Preheat the oven to 180°C, 350°F, Gas Mark 4.
2 Cook the rice with the cinnamon and citrus zests, uncovered, in plenty of boiling water for 10 minutes, then drain (don't rinse it). Pick out the cinnamon. Put the kettle on to boil.
3 Beat the eggs and egg whites together in a bowl, then beat in the milks and vanilla. With two spoons, stir in the rice until well combined.
4 Pour and scrape the rice into a 24 x 16 cm (9$^1/_2$ x 6$^1/_2$ inch) baking dish. Stand the dish in a larger baking dish or roasting tin, and pour enough boiling water into the larger dish or tin to come halfway up the sides of the smaller dish. Bake in the oven for about 45 minutes or until the custard is set, and the top is golden brown. Serve warm or at room temperature.

Rum and Raisin Bread and Unbutter Pudding

CALORIE COUNT 267 KCAL FAT CONTENT 2G PER SERVING

175 g (6 oz) sultanas

175 g (6 oz) raisins

1 tablespoon natural vanilla extract

2 tablespoons dark rum

2 tablespoons Amaretto de Saronno liqueur

450 ml (³/₄ pint) orange juice

grated or finely pared zest of 1 orange

¹/₂ cinnamon stick

150 g (5 oz) crustless fresh or one-day-old unsliced white
    bread, torn into rough pieces or cubed

2 whole eggs

3 egg whites

3 tablespoons lemon marmalade

3 tablespoons skimmed milk powder

500 ml (16 fl oz) skimmed milk

Serves 6–8

1 Preheat the oven to 180°C, 350°F, Gas Mark 4.
2 Put the sultanas and raisins, vanilla, rum, liqueur, orange juice, zest and
   cinnamon stick in a heavy-bottomed frying pan. Bring to the boil, then reduce
   the heat and simmer briskly for 5–7 minutes or until the fruit is plump and
   tender, and the liquid is absorbed. Set aside to cool.
3 Preheat the oven to 150°C, 300°F, Gas Mark 2. Put the kettle on to boil.
4 Put the bread into a large bowl. Put the whole eggs, egg whites and
   marmalade in a blender. Whisk the milk powder into the milk and pour into
   the blender. Blend until foamy.
5 Add the cooled fruit mixture to the bread (discard the cinnamon stick), and
   toss well together. Pour in the egg and milk mixture. With two spoons, gently
   turn the bread until it soaks up the liquid.
6 Pour and scrape the mixture into a baking dish (30 x 22 x 5 cm/12 x 8¹/₂ x 2
   inches). Stand the baking dish in a larger baking dish or roasting tin, and pour
   enough boiling water into the larger dish or tin to come halfway up the sides
   of the smaller dish. Bake in the oven for 50–60 minutes or until the pudding is
   puffed and golden. Remove the dish from the water and cool on a wire rack.
   Serve warm or at room temperature.

Chocolate Bread Pudding

CALORIE COUNT 288 KCAL FAT CONTENT 5G PER SERVING   (TRADITIONAL RECIPE CALORIE COUNT 957 KCAL FAT CONTENT 63G)

An indulgence of a pudding (each serving contains 15 g (^{1}/$_2$ oz) whole chocolate), best served warm, in large bowls, with a scoop of ice cream (try Coffee, Amaretti or Grape Nut Cinnamon Crunch, pages 102–3) melting on top. If you haven't any homemade ice cream, try a scoop of frozen low-fat vanilla yogurt from the supermarket.

175–200 g (6–7 oz) fresh or one-day-old white bread, sliced

405 g (13 oz) can sweetened condensed skimmed milk

175 ml (6 fl oz) skimmed milk

2 tablespoons low-fat unsweetened cocoa powder

^{1}/$_2$ tablespoon natural vanilla extract

2 whole eggs

3 egg whites

90 g (3 oz) high-cocoa-solid dark chocolate, roughly chopped

Serves 6–8

1 Cut each slice of bread in half on the diagonal, arrange the triangles in two overlapping rows in the bottom of a 30 x 22 x 5 cm (12 x 8^1/$_2$ x 2 inch) glass or ceramic baking dish.

2 Put the milks, cocoa powder, vanilla, eggs and egg whites in a blender, and blend until frothy. Add the chocolate, and pulse until it is finely chopped.

3 Pour the liquid over the bread, then, with a broad spatula, push the bread down into the liquid. Leave to soak for 1 hour, pushing the bread down into the liquid from time to time. Preheat the oven to 180°C, 350°F, Gas Mark 4. Put the kettle on to boil.

4 Stand the baking dish in a larger baking dish or roasting tin, and pour enough boiling water into the larger dish or tin to come halfway up the sides of the smaller dish. Bake in the oven for 45–55 minutes or until the pudding is puffed and set (a knife inserted near the centre will come out clean). Remove the dish from the water and leave to cool on a wire rack. Serve very warm or at room temperature.

Creamy Noodle Pudding

CALORIE COUNT 196 KCAL FAT CONTENT 5G PER SERVING   (TRADITIONAL RECIPE CALORIE COUNT 434 KCAL FAT CONTENT 21G)

This pudding looks like a beautiful tart, and each wedge shows off its noodle ribbons, nestled in creamy, sultana-studded, citrus-scented ricotta custard. This can be eaten warm, at room temperature or straight out of the fridge.

250 g (8 oz) broad egg noodles (Italian pantacce are perfect), roughly broken

pinch of salt

2 whole eggs

3 egg whites

125 g (4 oz) caster sugar

1 tablespoon natural vanilla extract

250 g (8 oz) carton ricotta

250 g (8 oz) carton quark

grated rind of ¹/₂ lemon and ¹/₂ orange

4 tablespoons sultanas

oil and water spray (page 10)

Serves 10–12

1 Preheat the oven to 180°C, 350°F, Gas Mark 4.
2 Cook the noodles with a pinch of salt in plenty of boiling water according to packet instructions or until just tender.
3 Meanwhile, beat together the eggs, egg whites and sugar until thickened and lemon-coloured. Beat in the vanilla, cheeses and citrus zests. Stir in the sultanas.
4 When the pasta is ready, drain it, rinse in cold water, and stir with your hands to separate. Add it to the creamy cheese mixture and toss with two spoons so everything is very well combined.
5 Spray a 23 cm (9 inch) springform tin with oil and water. Pour in the creamy noodles and smooth the top. Wrap the bottom of the pan in a sheet of kitchen foil, and put the tin into a larger roasting tin. Pour enough boiling water into the roasting tin to come halfway up the sides of the springform tin. (The foil prevents water seeping in.)
6 Bake in the oven for 40 minutes or until the pudding is just set. Cool on a wire rack for about 30 minutes, then loosen all around the edge of the pudding with a palette knife, and remove the sides of the tin.

CHAPTER 9

CHRISTMAS DESSERTS AND BAKING

Every year it comes around, and every year plenty of people shake in their boots at the thought of all that high-fat food, all those bilious nights, those pounds gained, that inevitable guilty January diet. Yes, it's fun and festive to eat well and copiously at Christmas, but why does it have to be so over-the-top rich and fatty? I'm not the food police; it's not my job to force everyone to follow a low-fat way of life whether they want to or not, but for those who long to do so, even in the face of Christmas's gastronomic overkill, I hope to offer a few alternatives. There is no law forcing us to over-consume during the holidays; holiday food can be just as festive, comforting and delicious *without* the fat dimension.

Christmas Cake

CALORIE COUNT 197 KCAL FAT CONTENT <0.5G PER SERVING   (TRADITIONAL RECIPE CALORIE COUNT 432 KCAL FAT CONTENT 5 G)

A beautifully dense, moist, fruity cake with all the flavours
of Christmas. I don't like glacé cherries, but many do, so add
them if you wish. This cake will keep for several days, but
not for weeks and months as a traditional fruit cake will. To
make it deliriously boozy, feed it once a day (see Note,
opposite).

375 g (12 oz) mixed dried fruit (sultanas, raisins, chopped
        mixed peel, currants)

175 ml (6 fl oz) orange juice

60 ml (2 fl oz) liqueur (choose between brandy, whisky,
        orange liqueur, Amaretto di Saronno, or a combination)

125 g (4 oz) glacé cherries, chopped (optional)

250 g (8 oz) tart eating apples, peeled, cored and diced

300 g (10 oz) self-raising flour

1 teaspoon ground cinnamon

3 teaspoons ground mixed spice

165 g (5¹/₂ oz) dark brown sugar

1 tablespoon black treacle

2 egg whites, lightly beaten

oil and water spray (page 10)

Serves 15

1 Preheat the oven to 160°C, 325°F, Gas Mark 3.
2 Combine the mixed fruit with the orange juice and liqueur in a glass bowl.
   Cover the bowl with cling film and cook in the microwave on full power for 5
   minutes. Pierce the film to release steam (avert your face and stand back), then
   uncover and stir. Re-cover and repeat as necessary until the mixture is tender,
   and of sticky, mincemeat consistency. (If you have no microwave, bake the
   mixture in a covered baking dish in the oven at 180°C, 350°F, Gas Mark 4 for 1
   hour, stirring halfway through, until the fruit is tender and of mincemeat
   consistency.)
3 Stir in the cherries (if using) and apples, and leave to cool thoroughly.
4 Sift the flour and spices together into a bowl. Add the sugar, black treacle and
   soaked fruit. Add the egg whites and mix very well.
5 Line a 20 cm (8 inch) non-stick round cake tin with greaseproof paper. Spray
   with oil and water. Scrape the mixture into the tin, smooth the top and bake in

the oven for 1¹/₂–2 hours. During the last hour of cooking, place a loose tent of foil over the top so that the cake does not overbrown. Check whether the cake is done by inserting a fine metal skewer in the centre. If it comes out clean, it is done. Leave the cake to cool in the tin on a wire rack before loosening it around the sides with a palette knife, and turning it out of the tin.

Note

When the cake has cooled, pierce it right through in several places with a fine skewer. Gently and evenly spoon 4–5 tablespoons brandy or liqueur (whatever you used in the fruit mix) over the cake. Wrap the cake well in foil. Repeat this step one more time the following morning, and each day until the cake is served. This 'feeding' results in a beautifully moist, boozy cake. What bliss!

Variation

Light Christmas Pudding

Steam the Christmas cake mix instead of baking it, for a very credible, very low-fat Christmas pudding. The pudding is so low in fat that it does not keep, so if you wish to make it some time before Christmas, wrap it well and freeze it. Re-steam it on the big day.

1 Prepare the Christmas Cake recipe from step 2 to the end of step 4.
2 Generously spray a 1.25 litre (2 pint) glass pudding basin with oil and water. Scrape the mixture into the basin. Top with a pleated piece of greaseproof paper, then with a pleated piece of foil, and tie well with string. Steam over boiling water for 3 hours, topping up the water as needed. Remove from the steamer and leave to cool.
3 When cooled, unwrap, then loosen the pudding from the basin very well all around with a flexible palette knife, using the knife to reach all the way down to the bottom of the basin, all around. Turn the basin over and shake the pudding out. Wrap well in a double thickness of foil and freeze.
4 The night before you plan to serve the pudding (Christmas Eve), take it out of the freezer and leave it, wrapped, on the counter, to thaw overnight. Next day, cover with greaseproof paper, tie well with string, and steam for 3 hours.

Chocolate–Orange Trifle

CALORIE COUNT 335 KCAL FAT CONTENT 2G PER SERVING

This is a formal, structured trifle, quite different from the higgledy-piggledy trifle on page 55. Use the leftover angel cake for additional festive desserts during the holiday period. The cake cubes nestle in fresh orange jelly under a layer of dark chocolate pudding. If you hate the idea of a jelly layer, leave it out, and lightly sprinkle the cake cubes with a mixture of orange juice and Cointreau instead. This trifle looks fabulous and feeds a crowd.

Sponge
250 g (8 oz) Vanilla Angel Cake (page 20)

Orange Jelly
600 ml (1 pint) fresh orange juice
2 sachets (1 tablespoon each) powdered gelatine
100 g (3^1/$_2$ oz) caster sugar
125 ml (4 fl oz) orange-flavoured liqueur (e.g. Cointreau or Grand Marnier)
125 ml (4 fl oz) sweet white wine (e.g. Riesling)

Makes one 3 litre (5 pint) trifle; serves 10

Cut the cake into cubes and place in a single layer in the bottom of a 3 litre (5 pint) glass bowl.

1 Warm 350 ml (12 fl oz) of the orange juice in a saucepan, remove from the heat and sprinkle over the gelatine. Leave for 5 minutes to soften.
2 Bring the remaining orange juice to the boil in another saucepan, then remove from the heat and add the sugar. Stir until the sugar has dissolved, then stir in the orange liqueur and wine. Stir into the gelatine mixture, then leave to cool until barely warm.
3 Pour the gelatine mixture over the cake cubes. Very gently stir them together, so that the cake is thoroughly soaked but doesn't disintegrate. Chill in the refrigerator until completely set. (This takes several hours, and can be done overnight, for convenience.)

Chocolate Pudding Layer
1 quantity Old-Fashioned Dark Chocolate Pudding (page 109)

Make up a batch of Old-Fashioned Dark Chocolate Pudding and leave to cool with a covering of non-PVC (microwave) cling film right on its surface. When barely cool, swirl it evenly over the set jelly. Cover again with a piece of cling film right on its surface, then chill in the refrigerator for several hours.

Topping: Orange-Vanilla Cream
1/2 teaspoon natural vanilla extract

2 generous tablespoons orange marmalade

500 g (1 lb) very low-fat fromage frais

1 tablespoon low-fat unsweetened cocoa powder

1/2–1 tablespoon icing sugar

canned mandarin segments, drained, to decorate

1 Whisk the vanilla extract and the orange marmalade into the fromage frais and swirl over the set chocolate layer.
2 Combine the cocoa and icing sugar in a bowl and sift it evenly over the surface of the trifle. Refrigerate until needed. At serving time, decorate with mandarin segments.

Note

If you don't want to take time to bake an Angel Cake, use trifle sponges (made with whole eggs, but no added fat) and tear each sponge into 2-3 pieces.

Overleaf: Sweet Potato and Ginger Custard Torte with Mango and Cranberry Compote (pages 86-87)

Left: Meringue Layer Torte filled with Amaretti Cherry Cheesecake Mousse and stoned, halved cherries macerated in Amaretto di Saronno (page 63)

Chocolate–Cherry Trifle

CALORIE COUNT 414 KCAL FAT CONTENT 2G PER SERVING

Another trifle extravaganza to feed a crowd, with a milk chocolate layer this time, and a base of cherry jelly.

Sponge
250 g (8 oz) Chocolate Angel Cake (page 21)

Cut the cake into cubes and arrange in a single layer in the bottom of a 3 litre (5 pint) glass bowl.

Cherry Jelly
3 x 300 g (10 oz) can stoned black cherries in natural juice (or use stoned cherries in sweetened juice, and omit the sugar)

2 sachets (1 tablespoon each) powdered gelatine

100 g (3^1/$_2$ oz) caster sugar

125 ml (4 fl oz) sweet white wine (e.g. Riesling)

125 ml (4 fl oz) Amaretto di Saronno

Makes one 3 litre (5 pint) trifle; serves 10

1 Drain the juice from the cherries into a jug. If necessary, add enough water to the juice to make it up to 350 ml (12 fl oz) liquid.
2 Heat the cherry juice until warm, then transfer 175 ml (6 fl oz) to a measuring jug. Sprinkle over the gelatine and leave to soften. Bring the rest of the juice to the boil and add the sugar, stirring until dissolved.
3 Stir the wine and Amaretto into the cherry juice and sugar solution, then stir into the cherry juice and gelatine mixture. Cool until barely warm, then stir in the cherries.
4 Pour the cherry mixture over the cake cubes, and stir gently so that the cake is thoroughly soaked but does not disintegrate. Chill in the refrigerator until completely set. (This takes several hours, and can be done overnight, for convenience.)

Creamy Chocolate Layer

950 ml (32 fl oz) skimmed milk

90 g (3 oz) skimmed milk powder

8 tablespoons low-fat unsweetened cocoa powder

175 ml (6 fl oz) water

2 sachets (1 tablespoon each) powdered gelatine

pinch of salt

175 g (6 oz) caster sugar

500 g (1 lb) very low-fat fromage frais

1 Whisk together the milk, milk powder and cocoa. Rinse a heavy-bottomed saucepan with cold water. Do not dry it. Bring the milk and chocolate mixture to just below boiling in the saucepan. Meanwhile, heat the water until warm in another saucepan, then remove from the heat and sprinkle over the gelatine. Leave for 5 minutes to soften.

2 When the chocolate milk is just forming bubbles at the edges, remove from the heat and add the salt and sugar. Stir until dissolved. Stir in the softened gelatine and water, then cool to room temperature.

3 Fold and stir the fromage frais and the milk mixture together, then whisk gently until smooth. Pour the mixture through a sieve (rub it through with a rubber spatula) into a bowl and leave to cool until barely warm. Pour this mixture over the thoroughly set jelly and chill for several hours until the chocolate custard is set.

Honeyed Almond Cream Topping

1 teaspoon natural almond extract

2 tablespoons mild runny honey

500 g (1 lb) very low-fat fromage frais

drained canned cherries and crushed amaretti biscuits to decorate

1 Stir the almond extract and the honey into the fromage frais.

2 Swirl this mixture evenly over the set custard and refrigerate until needed. At serving time, decorate with cherries and crushed amaretti biscuits.

Mincemeat

CALORIE COUNT 21 KCAL FAT CONTENT NEG PER TABLESPOON

Mincemeat (the traditional version) contains suet or vegetable suet. This is the simplest mincemeat imaginable: plenty of dried fruit and peel, a slosh of booze, and some spice. It will keep for several weeks in the fridge.

500 g (1 lb) mixed dried sultanas, raisins, currants, candied orange and lemon peel (the peel chopped into tiny pieces with scissors)

270 g (9 oz) package ready-to-eat dried apricots, coarsely chopped with scissors

150 g (5 oz) package dried apple chunks, coarsely chopped with scissors

1/2 teaspoon each of ground cinnamon, ground allspice and grated nutmeg

1 vanilla pod

60 ml (2 fl oz) each of medium sherry, brandy and Cointreau

125 ml (4 fl oz) water

Makes 1.5 litres (2 1/2 pints)

1 Preheat the oven to 180°C, 350°F, Gas Mark 4.
2 Combine all the ingredients in a baking dish, cover tightly and bake for about 1 hour or until the fruit is tender and of a sticky mincemeat consistency. Remove the vanilla pod before using. (Rinse and dry the pod; it can be re-used.)

Variation

Microwave Mincemeat

1 Combine all the ingredients in a bowl and mix together well.
2 Transfer the mixture to a 1.8 litre (3 pint) glass measuring jug and cover with a plate. Microwave on full power for 4 minutes. Carefully uncover, averting your face from the hot steam, and stir.
3 Re-cover and microwave on full power for 2–3 minutes more. Repeat, as necessary, stirring each time, until the fruit is tender and of a sticky mincemeat consistency. Remove the vanilla pod before using the mincemeat. (Rinse and dry the pod; it can be re-used.)

Mincemeat Tartlets

CALORIE COUNT 70 KCAL FAT CONTENT <0.5G PER TARTLET   (TRADITIONAL RECIPE CALORIE COUNT 306 KCAL FAT CONTENT 16G)

The components of these adorable alternative mince pies can be made well ahead of time, but only fill them just before serving or they will go soggy. The little bread cases are filled with a soft, milky vanilla pudding, and topped with mincemeat. I give two versions of the vanilla pudding – one for making in the microwave, one on the hob.

> Tartlet Shells (page 143)
> Mincemeat (page 132)
> Vanilla Milk Pudding (page 135)

> Makes 12

Fill each tartlet shell with a dollop of vanilla pudding, and top with a dab of mincemeat. Serve at once.

Note

Wondrous selections of dried fruit can be found on the supermarket shelves these days. Feel free to enliven your mincemeat with exotic and non-traditional ingredients. Dried cherries, cranberries and blueberries work very well. If you use a good measure of these, substitute cherry or blueberry cream (page 150) for the milk pudding. (Fill the tartlet shells with the mincemeat, then top with a tiny blob of the cream.) And why not try a bit of dried mango, papaya and pineapple in your mincemeat? Use a slosh of lychee liqueur and rum instead of sherry and brandy.

Mincemeat Turnovers

CALORIE COUNT 89 KCAL FAT CONTENT <1G PER TURNOVER

Filo turnovers can be made in advance up to the baking point, and refrigerated for a few days, or frozen for a few months.

1 package filo, thawed

1 egg, lightly beaten, or 2 lightly beaten egg whites, or oil spray (use a pure oil spray, not oil and water)

Mincemeat (page 132)

Makes about 12

1 Preheat the oven to 190°C, 375°F, Gas Mark 5.
2 Put a sheet of cling film on your work surface. Unwrap the filo, unfold it, and place it on the cling film. Working from top to bottom, with a sharp knife, cut the stack of pastry crossways in two. Immediately cover both stacks with another sheet of cling film.
3 Spread out one piece of filo on a clean surface. (Keep the rest well covered; it dries out very quickly.) With a pastry brush, lightly coat the filo piece with egg or egg white, or spray with oil. Fold the top third of the piece down and the bottom third up as if folding a business letter.
4 Place a generous tablespoon of mincemeat on the lower right-hand corner of the filo piece. Fold down the top right-hand corner to form a triangle and cover the mincemeat. Brush with egg or spray with oil. Fold back up to form a new triangle. Continue folding up and down until you have formed a compact, many-layered triangle. Brush the finished triangle lightly with egg, or spray with oil, and place on a *non-stick* baking tray. Continue until all the mincemeat has been used up. (At this point, the turnovers may be refrigerated for a day or two, or frozen for months.)
5 Bake the turnovers in the oven for 20–30 minutes, or until puffed up and golden. If baking from frozen, add an extra 5 minutes to the baking time. Serve at once.

Microwave Vanilla Milk Pudding

CALORIE COUNT 181 KCAL FAT CONTENT <0.5G PER ¼ PINT

5 tablespoons skimmed milk powder

3 tablespoons cornflour

4 tablespoons sugar

pulp of 1 vanilla pod (page14)

about 500 ml (18 fl oz) skimmed milk (1 long-life carton)

Makes 600 ml (1 pint); serves 4

1 Put the milk powder, cornflour, sugar and vanilla into a 2.1 litre (3½ pint), 18 cm (7 inch) top diameter, Pyrex clear glass measuring jug.

2 With a wire whisk, whisk the milk into the dry ingredients. Whisk well – you don't want lumps – and vigorous whisking reduces the risk of volcanic eruptions in the microwave. Cover the bowl with a plate.

3 Microwave on full power for 3 minutes. Carefully remove the plate, averting your face from the hot steam and whisk thoroughly. Re-cover and microwave for another 2 minutes. Carefully uncover and whisk again, then re-cover and microwave for a final 1½–2 minutes or until boiled, thickened and smooth.

4 Whisk and leave to stand for 3–4 minutes. Store in the refrigerator, covered with a sheet of non-PVC (microwave) cling film directly on the surface of the sauce.

'Life is seldom what it seems,
Skimmed milk masquerades as cream.'

W. S. Gilbert

Alternative Vanilla Milk Pudding

CALORIE COUNT 168 KCAL FAT CONTENT <0.5G PER 1/2 PINT

Bring the milk to the boil gently as it easily scorches.

500 ml (16 fl oz) skimmed milk
45 g (1¹/₂ oz) skimmed milk powder
1 vanilla pod
1¹/₂ sachets (1¹/₂ tablespoons) powdered gelatine
125 ml (4 fl oz) water
pinch of salt
125 g (4 oz) caster sugar
500 g (1 lb) very low-fat fromage frais

Makes 1 litre (1³/₄ pints); serves 7

1 Whisk together the milk and milk powder. Rinse a heavy-bottomed, non-stick saucepan with water. Pour the water out but don't dry the pan. (This helps reduce the chance of scorching.)

2 Put the milk in the rinsed-out saucepan. Split open the vanilla pod and scrape the pulp into the milk (throw in the scooped-out pod as well). Gently and slowly bring the milk to just below the boil (tiny bubbles will form around the edge). Meanwhile, heat the water until warm in another saucepan, then remove from the heat and sprinkle over the gelatine. Leave for 5 minutes to soften.

3 Remove the milk from the heat and add the salt and sugar. Stir until dissolved. Stir in the softened gelatine and water, then cool to room temperature.

4 Whisk the fromage frais and the milk mixture together, then pour the mixture through a sieve (rub it through with a rubber spatula) into a bowl. Chill for several hours or overnight.

Christmas Bread and Unbutter Pudding

CALORIE COUNT 221KCAL FAT CONTENT 3 G PER SERVING   (TRADITIONAL RECIPE CALORIE COUNT 363 KCAL FAT CONTENT 24G)

This bread pudding is bursting at the seams with all the flavours of Christmas. It makes a great holiday pudding or brunch dish.

175–250 g (6–8 oz) 1–2-day-old good-quality white bread
175 g (6 oz) Mincemeat (page 132)
2 whole eggs
3 egg whites
3 tablespoons orange marmalade
3 tablespoons skimmed milk powder
500 ml (16 fl oz) skimmed milk
1 teaspoon natural vanilla extract
1–2 good pinches ground cinnamon or mixed spice

Serves 6

1 Cut the bread into slices, then cut the slices into quarters. Arrange in two overlapping rows in the bottom of a 20 x 30 cm (8 x 12 inch) glass or ceramic baking dish. Scatter the mincemeat in between, under and over the bread slices.

2 Put the eggs and egg whites in a blender with the marmalade, and blend to combine. Whisk the milk powder into the milk, then whisk in the vanilla and spice. Pour into the blender and blend until foamy. Pour the mixture over the bread and mincemeat. Use a broad spatula to push the bread down into the liquid. Leave to stand, occasionally pushing the bread into the liquid, while you preheat the oven to 180°C, 350°F, Gas Mark 4. Put the kettle on to boil.

3 Choose a baking dish or roasting tin larger than the one in which you have made the pudding, and put it in the preheated oven. Put the pudding dish in the larger dish or tin, and pour enough boiling water into the larger dish to come about halfway up the sides of the pudding dish. Bake for 45–55 minutes or until the pudding is puffed and firm. (A knife inserted near the centre will emerge clean.)

4 Remove the baking dish from the water bath and leave to cool on a wire rack. Serve warm or at room temperature.

Bûche De Noel

CALORIE COUNT 220KCAL FAT CONTENT 5G PER SERVING   (TRADITIONAL RECIPE CALORIE COUNT 331 KCAL FAT CONTENT 21G)

No one will know that this is a low-fat dessert. If you are *very* clever, you might try your hand at meringue mushrooms, lightly dusted with cocoa powder, as decoration. You won't need all the chocolate spread for the icing; you can use what's left over in many other ways throughout the holiday.

1 Chocolate Angel Sheet Cake (page 23)

Filling
  Chocolate Chestnut Spread (page 116) or Orange Cream (page 150)

Icing
  Old-Fashioned Dark Chocolate Spread (page 109)
  15 g ('/₂ oz) high-cocoa-solid dark chocolate, grated

Serves 10

1 When the angel sheet cake is cool, spread a clean tea towel on the work surface, and turn the cooled cake out on to it. Carefully peel off the lining paper.
2 With a palette knife, spread the sponge with the filling of your choice. Starting at a long edge, and using the tea towel to help, roll up the cake. It may crack, but it won't matter – the finished roll will still look just fine, and taste glorious.
3 Spread the rolled cake roughly with Chocolate Spread, giving it a bark-like appearance. Sprinkle with the grated chocolate. Store the roll, loosely covered, in the refrigerator, until required.

Note
To ensure a crack-free roulade, fill and roll it while it is still quite fresh, just give it a chance to cool somewhat, slather on the filling and roll carefully. Having said that, it is sometimes convenient to make the cake a day ahead of time, then fill, roll and ice it on the next day. If it does crack, it really won't matter – it just adds to the rough, rustic log-like quality of the final roulade.

CHAPTER 10

BASICS AND MISCELLANEOUS

All the basic recipes needed throughout this book are in this chapter: pie and tart crusts, sauces, creams, and so on. Some of them can be mixed and matched to form glorious desserts in their own right: one of the creams, for instance, paired with one of the sauces, purées or compotes, and decorated with a halved almond biscuit; or one of the creams can be drained to make it thicker, swirled into a crumb crust, and topped with glazed fruit or a fruit compote.

Crumb Crusts

These are the bases for cheesecakes, cheese pies and so on. They are based on the classic Graham Cracker (or Digestive biscuit) crust made from crumbs, butter and sugar.

Amaretti-Flavoured Crumb Crust

CALORIE COUNT 1215 KCAL FAT CONTENT 9G PER WHOLE RECIPE

oil spray
150 g (5 oz) amaretti biscuits
150 g (5 oz) Grape Nuts cereal
4 egg whites
oil and water spray

Makes one 25 cm (10 inch) crust

1 Preheat the oven to 180°C, 350°F, Gas Mark 4.
2 Put the dry ingredients in a blender or food processor and process to coarse crumbs. Tip into a bowl.
3 Lightly beat the egg whites, and mix with the crumbs until thoroughly combined.
4 Lightly spray a 25 cm (10 inch) round non-stick flan tin or springform tin with oil spray. Scrape the crumb mixture into the tin and, with the back of a serving spoon, spread it evenly over the bottom and up the sides.
5 Bake in the oven for 7–10 minutes, then leave to cool in the tin on a wire rack.

Varaitions
• Use all Grape Nuts (no amaretti).
• For a chocolate base, add 1 teaspoon low-fat unsweetened cocoa powder in step 2.

Rice Pie Crust

CALORIE COUNT 1092 KCAL FAT CONTENT 4G PER WHOLE RECIPE

Rice makes a good base for family dessert tarts. Make this
on the day you plan to use it – rice does not keep well.

270 g (9 oz) Jasmine rice
¹/₂ vanilla pod, cut into 4 pieces
grated zest of ¹/₂ orange and ¹/₂ lemon
1 cinnamon stick, broken
2 egg whites, lightly beaten
2 tablespoons orange blossom honey
oil and water spray (page 10)

Makes one 28 cm (11 inch) crust

1 Cook the rice in plenty of boiling water with the vanilla pod, citrus zests and
  cinnamon stick for 10 minutes. Drain well, (do not rinse) and cool. Remove the
  pieces of vanilla pod and cinnamon. (The vanilla pod can be rinsed, dried and
  re-used.)
2 Preheat the oven to 220°C, 425°F, Gas Mark 7. Combine the egg whites, honey
  and rice in a large bowl, and toss with two spoons to mix thoroughly and to
  break up the clumps of rice.
3 Spray a 28 cm (11 inch) non-stick flan dish with oil and water, then tip the rice
  into the dish. Use the back of a large spoon to spread it evenly over the
  bottom and up the sides of the dish.
4 Bake in the oven for 20 minutes or until set and crisp around the edge, then
  leave to cool in the dish on a wire rack for a few minutes. Gently loosen all
  around the sides and bottom with a palette knife to ease serving later.

Note

I love this but it is somewhat unusual; that's why I suggest it for family
feasting rather than dinner party fare. I tried it with brown rice once, and it
was just too dull and worthy. If you wish, you could use a meringue pie crust
(page 66) instead of the unusual rice one (not nearly as healthy and nutritious,
I hasten to add). Just fill it right before serving.

Almond Biscuits

CALORIE COUNT 61 KCAL FAT CONTENT <1G PER SERVING

These 'recycled' biscuits (ground up amaretti mixed with Grape Nuts to make new biscuits) have a crunchy quality that I like very much. Eat them as they are, or use in the 'deconstructed cheesecake' (see page 49).

oil spray
75 g (2^{1}/$_{2}$ oz) amaretti biscuits
75 g (2^{1}/$_{2}$ oz) Grape Nuts cereal
2 egg whites

Makes 10

1 Preheat the oven to 180°C, 350°F, Gas Mark 4.
2 Put the dry ingredients into a blender or food processor and process to coarse crumbs. Tip into a bowl.
3 Lightly beat the egg whites and mix with the crumb mixture until thoroughly combined.
4 Lightly spray a non-stick baking sheet with oil. Spoon tablespoons of the crumb mixture on to the oiled baking sheet, leaving spaces between. Flatten them with the back of the spoon.
5 Bake in the oven for 7–10 minutes, then leave to cool on the baking sheet on a wire rack. When cool, loosen all around with a palette knife. Refrigerate until needed.

Variation

Chocolate Dipped Biscuits

1 Add 1 teaspoon low-fat unsweetened cocoa powder in step 2.
2 Dip the cooled biscuits halfway into melted high-cocoa-solid dark chocolate (see page 107).

Tartlet Shells

CALORIE COUNT 86 KCAL FAT CONTENT <1G PER SERVING

These adorable little bread cases can be filled with one of the 'creams' (see pages 150–54) and topped with a little fruit compote (dried or cooked fresh) or a few fresh berries. Fill them just before serving; if they sit around they will go soggy.

12 slices top-quality sliced bakery bread, white or brown
90–125 ml (3–4 fl oz) fresh orange juice

Makes 12

1 Preheat the oven to 150°C, 300°F, Gas Mark 2.
2 With a 7.5 cm (3 inch) diameter drinking glass, cut a circle out of the centre of each slice of bread. Flatten each circle with a rolling pin. (Save all trimmings for breadcrumbs, bread puddings, etc.)
3 Press a round of bread into each cup in a 12-section non-stick bun tin. With your fingers, mould the bread down and up the sides of the cups.
4 Bake in the oven for 15 minutes, then lightly brush the interior of each bread shell with orange juice. Remove the shells from the bun tin and bake directly on the oven shelf for about 10 minutes more, until totally dried right through, turning them once or twice. Cool on a wire rack, then store in an airtight container (they will keep for weeks).

Variation

Bread Base for Simple Fruit Tarts

Instead of moulding circles of bread in a bun tin (as above), you can bake them flat until dried right through, and then use to make simple fruit tarts. Using a glass, cup or small bowl as a template, cut circles from slices of excellent-quality white bread. Each circle will form the base of a single tart. Dry the bread on a baking sheet in the oven, as above, until dried through (but not browned). Leave to cool as above, and store in an airtight container. To serve, heap one of the fruit compotes on the bases (the compote used as a crumble base, page 71, works well) and top with a blob of one of the 'creams' (see pages 150–54).

Sauces

Raspberry Coulis

CALORIE COUNT 6 KCAL FAT CONTENT NEG PER TABLESPOON

One of the easiest, the most vivid, and the most delicious of dessert sauces has also become one of the most clichéd, but that takes nothing away from its beauty and versatility.

2 x 375 g (12 oz) packages frozen raspberries, thawed
icing sugar
a few drops of lemon juice, if needed

Makes 500 ml (16 fl oz)

1 Drain the berries and purée the fruit in a food processor or blender. Press the purée through a nylon sieve to eliminate the pips.
2 Sweeten the purée with icing sugar to taste. Add a few drops of lemon juice, if necessary, to sharpen the taste. Refrigerate until needed.

Mango Sauce

CALORIE COUNT 10 KCAL FAT CONTENT NEG PER TABLESPOON

If your supermarket doesn't have ready-to-eat chunks, peel and cube two fresh ripe mangoes instead (see below).

250 g (8 oz) package ready-cut mango chunks
1 teaspoon natural vanilla extract
1 tablespoon Cointreau

Makes 300 ml ($^1/_2$ pint)

Put all the ingredients in a blender, and blend to perfect smoothness.

To Peel and Dice a Mango
1 With a sharp knife, cut the mango as if you were slicing it lengthways in half, but cutting just to one side of the large, flat central stone to remove one 'cheek'. Repeat on the other side of the stone to cut off the second 'cheek'.

2 With a small, sharp knife, score each mango half lengthways and crossways, cutting through the flesh all the way to, but not through, the skin. Push in the skin as if you were turning the mango half inside out. The mango flesh will stand out in cubes. Cut these cubes off the skin.

3 Peel the skin from the centre slice left on the stone, then slice the mango flesh off the stone and use the trimmings in the sauce.

Blueberry Sauce

CALORIE COUNT 13 KCAL FAT CONTENT NEG PER TABLESPOON

Now that frozen blueberries are readily available, you can have a bracing dose of blue food anytime you want. Blueberries, lemon and cinnamon are a magical combo; serve this with ice cream, berries, or swirled into very low-fat fromage frais or sweetened drained yogurt (page 149). Garnish with fresh blueberries.

250 g (8 oz) package frozen blueberries, thawed
1/2 lemon, sliced (remove the pips)
1/2 cinnamon stick
1 teaspoon natural vanilla extract
2–3 teaspoons caster sugar, to taste
a few drops of orange and lemon juice

Makes 150 ml (5 fl oz)

1 Purée the berries with their juices in a blender, then push through a nylon sieve.

2 Put the purée in a small saucepan with the remaining ingredients and bring to a simmer. Taste, and add a little more sugar or citrus juice, as needed. Simmer for 4–5 minutes, then remove from the heat, transfer to a bowl, cool and chill.

3 Before serving, strain the sauce and discard the cinnamon stick and lemon slices.

Compotes

Both these compotes can be used as fruit sauces, or as puddings in their own right. Sprinkle a crumb topping on the surface and bake (see page 71), and they become crumbles.

Peach Compote

CALORIE COUNT 370 KCAL FAT CONTENT 1G PER WHOLE RECIPE

750 g (1½ lb) ripe peaches (peeled) or nectarines
juice of 1 orange and ½ lemon
1 tablespoon each of Cointreau and natural vanilla extract
2 tablespoons peach preserves
1 tablespoon cornflour
honey (optional)
a few drops of lemon juice (optional)

Makes 600 ml (1 pint)

1 Preheat the oven to 190°C, 375°F, Gas Mark 5.
2 Cut the peaches or nectarines into chunks over a bowl to catch the juices. Put the fruit chunks and all the other ingredients, except the honey and lemon juice, in the bowl with the juices, then transfer to a baking dish. Bake, uncovered, in the oven for about 30 minutes, stirring occasionally, until bubbling and thickened. Taste and add a little honey and/or a few drops of lemon juice, if needed.

Hunza Apricot Puree

CALORIE COUNT 24 KCAL FAT CONTENT NEG PER TABLESPOON

Dried Hunza apricots are beige, ugly and as hard as little boulders. Get past this – it doesn't matter. When cooked, they will knock your socks off with their intense, aromatic, honeyed sweetness. It's hard work pushing the apricots through a sieve, but it is very much worth the effort. I use the purée in baking, in fools (swirl it into very low-fat fromage frais or drained yogurt), and drizzled on meringues. It is quite addictive. It will keep in the fridge for a week, or you can freeze it in usable amounts.

> **500 g (1 lb) dried Hunza apricots**
> **about 900 ml (1 1/2 pints) water**
> **1 tablespoon natural vanilla extract**

Makes 500 ml (16 fl oz)

1 Put the apricots in a non-stick frying pan with the water and vanilla. Simmer for about 30 minutes or until the apricots are very tender (falling apart) and the liquid almost gone. (Add more water, if needed, as the apricots cook.)
2 Push the apricots through a sieve and discard the stones. Store in the fridge.

Blueberry Compote

CALORIE COUNT 409 KCAL FAT CONTENT 2G PER WHOLE RECIPE

> **500 g (1 lb) blueberries**
> **3–4 tablespoons caster sugar**
> **1 tablespoon cornflour**
> **1/2 teaspoon natural vanilla extract**
> **1/2 tablespoon lemon juice**
> **juice of 1/2 orange**
> **pinch each of ground cinnamon and grated nutmeg**

Makes 300 ml (1/2 pint)

1 Preheat the oven to 190°C, 375°F, Gas Mark 5.
2 Mix all the ingredients together in a bowl, then transfer to a baking dish and bake, uncovered, in the oven for 15–20 minutes or until most of the blueberries have popped, and the mixture is thick, bubbly and juicy.

Dried Apricot Puree

CALORIE COUNT 18 KCAL FAT CONTENT NEG PER TABLESPOON

This purée is not as piercingly aromatic and flavourful as the Hunza variety, but very good none the less, and a good filling for a pair of meringues or for crêpes (see page 84). Because the apricots are stoned, and therefore do not need to be pushed laboriously through a sieve, this purée is much easier to prepare than Hunza Apricot Purée.

500 g (1 lb) ready-to-eat dried apricots
about 900 ml (1 1/2 pints) water
1 tablespoon natural vanilla extract
1 tablespoon Cointreau
a few drops of lemon juice
about 1 tablespoon orange blossom honey (if needed)

Makes 750 ml (1 1/4 pints)

1 Put the apricots in a non-stick frying pan with the water and vanilla. Simmer for about 30 minutes or until the apricots are very tender (falling apart) and the liquid almost gone. (Add more water, if needed, as the apricots cook.)
2 Purée the apricots in a food processor with the Cointreau, lemon juice and honey (if it is needed). Store in the fridge.

Prune Puree

CALORIE COUNT 21 KCAL FAT CONTENT NEG PER TABLESPOON

If you can't find the new-fangled 'Lighter Bake' (see page 28), make your own prune purée.

250 g (8 oz) ready-to-eat stoned prunes
6 tablespoons water

Makes 250 ml (8 fl oz)

Put the prunes and water in a food processor, and process until the prunes are puréed. (It will not be perfectly smooth but that's okay.)

Drained Yogurt

Very low-fat yogurt is thin and watery, but it can be drained in a sieve lined with dampened butter muslin or a dampened J-cloth until it is as thick as Greek yogurt. Use a blue J-cloth only; the pink ones leak dye.

very low-fat natural yogurt

1 Line a sieve with a double layer of dampened butter muslin or a dampened jelly bag, or with a dampened blue J-cloth. Place over a large bowl. Pour the yogurt into the sieve, fold the ends of the cloth over the top and refrigerate overnight. (For a creamier result, refrigerate for 2–3 hours only.)
2 On the next day, drain the liquid from the bowl (it can be used as part of the liquid in bread baking), and rinse and dry the bowl. Scrape the drained yogurt into the bowl.

Creams

No need to long for whipped cream, mascarpone cheese, crème fraîche and clotted cream; ricotta, very low-fat fromage frais, quark or drained yogurt (or combinations of these) can be whisked with various sweeteners to make gorgeous clouds of cream topping for your puddings.

Orange Cream

CALORIE COUNT 215 KCAL FAT CONTENT 9G PER ¼ PINT

Ricotta has a milky sweetness to it; quark is a bit tart. A combination of the two works very well. Of course, all quark is virtually non-fat.

500 g (1 lb) quark or ricotta, or a combination

2 heaped tablespoons orange marmalade or no-added-sugar, high-fruit orange spread

1 teaspoon natural vanilla extract

1 tablespoon orange-flavoured liqueur (Grand Marnier or Cointreau)

Makes 450 ml (³/₄ pint)

Put all the ingredients in a food processor, and process until well mixed and fluffy.

Variations

Substitute other marmalades, jams, conserves or spreads for the orange, for instance: wild blueberry conserve; black cherry conserve; apricot no-added-sugar, high-fruit spread; peach conserve; lemon shred marmalade.

Honey Vanilla Cream

CALORIE COUNT 104 KCAL FAT CONTENT <0.5G PER '/, PINT

1 vanilla pod or $^1/_2$–1 tablespoon natural vanilla extract
500 g (1 lb) very low-fat fromage frais or drained yogurt
(page 149)
2 tablespoons runny honey

Makes 550 ml (18 fl oz)

1 If using a vanilla pod, split it open lengthways with a small, sharp knife. With the tip of the knife, scrape the soft pulp from each half into the fromage frais. (Save the scraped pod to store in a canister of caster sugar or to simmer in dried fruit compote.)
2 Whisk the honey into the fromage frais. Stir so that the black vanilla bean specks are evenly distributed through the fromage frais. If you are using vanilla extract, whisk it in. Store in the refrigerator.

Variation

Maple Cream

Substitute maple syrup for the honey.

Lemon Brown Sugar Cream

CALORIE COUNT 118 KCAL FAT CONTENT <0.5G PER ¹/₄ PINT

If you make this just before you serve it, the cream will be
studded with crunchy bits of sugar (lovely!). Make it ahead
of time, and the sugar will dissolve; still lovely, but no
crunch.

500 g (1 lb) carton very low-fat fromage frais
1 small lemon, scrubbed
about 1¹/₂ tablespoons demerara sugar

Makes 500 ml (16 fl oz)

1 Zest the lemon over the fromage frais, so that both the grated zest and the
  lemon oil go in.
2 Swirl the sugar into the fromage frais so that the cream is speckled with little
  bits of melting sugar.

Note

If you have brown sugar cubes on hand there is a better way to make Lemon
Brown Sugar Cream. Rub one or two of the cubes all over the skin of an
unwaxed lemon, turning the cube so that it is thoroughly imbued with lemon
oil. Crumble the cube into the fromage frias.

Cannoli Cream

CALORIE COUNT 398 KCAL FAT CONTENT 19G PER ³/₄ PINT

This candied-peel-studded cream is meant to fill the cake on page 26, but I have also used it as the cream layer for a truly splendid tiramisù. (Of course, you have to like candied peel.) If you can find a source of Italian candied fruits, use them in place of the peel.

30 g (1 oz) candied lemon peel
30 g (1 oz) candied orange peel
2 tablespoons sultanas
125 ml (4 fl oz) Marsala or medium sherry
125 ml (4 fl oz) orange juice
1 tablespoon natural vanilla extract
2 x 250 g (8 oz) carton ricotta
250 g (8 oz) carton quark
1–2 tablespoons orange marmalade

Makes 450 ml (³/₄ pint)

1 Chop the candied peel into very small dice (use scissors) and put it into a frying pan with the sultanas, Marsala or sherry, orange juice and vanilla. Simmer until the fruits are plump and tender and bathed in a scant, syrupy sauce. Cool.

2 Put the ricotta and quark in a food processor. Add the syrupy fruit mixture and marmalade, and process until the fruit-studded cheese is very smooth and fluffy.

Ginger Cream

CALORIE COUNT 32 KCAL FAT CONTENT 18G PER ¼ PINT

I love gingery desserts, especially when the ginger is paired with a creamy texture. Imagine this topping a warm Apple and Pear Compote (page 71) or filling a Chocolate Roulade (page 27).

2 x 250 g (8 oz) carton ricotta

250 g (8 oz) carton quark

1 piece stem ginger, very finely chopped (use scissors)

3–4 lumps crystallised ginger, very finely chopped (use scissors)

1 tablespoon syrup from jar of stem ginger

1–2 tablespoons ginger conserve

½ tablespoon natural vanilla extract

Makes 450 ml (¾ pint)

1 Combine all the ingredients in a food processor, and process until very smooth and fluffy.
2 Taste, and add a little more conserve or ginger syrup, if required. Refrigerate until needed.

Marmalade Glaze

Melt some marmalade or jam in a frying pan or small saucepan with a little orange-flavoured liqueur (Cointreau or Grand Marnier) or water. Use a pastry brush to brush it on cake layers.

MAIL ORDER GUIDE

Terence Fisher
Chocolate Wholesaler
Earl Soham Business Centre
Earl Soham
Woodbridge
Suffolk
IP13 7SA
Tel: 01728 685955
Fax: 01728 685956

Low fat unsweetened cocoa powder
Excellent quality high-cocoa-solids
    dark chocolate

Lakeland Plastics
Alexandra Buildings
Windermere
Cumbria
LA23 1BQ
Tel: 015394 88100
Fax: 015394 88300

Bakeware
Pure natural vanilla extract
Pure natural lemon and almond
    extracts
Chocolate extract

Made in America
Hathaway Retail Park
Chippenham
SN15 1JG
Tel: 01249 447558
Fax: 01249 446142

Oil sprays
Pure natural vanilla extract

Divertimenti
45–47 Wigmore Street
London
W1H 9LE
Tel: 0171 935 0689
Fax: 0171 224 0058

Bakeware
Angel cake tins
Cheesecake tins

INDEX

References in **bold** indicate complete recipes